MATT AND TOM OLDFIELD

ULTIMATE
FOOTBALL HEROES

DE GEA

FROM THE PLAYGROUND
TO THE PITCH

D1102878

DINO

Published by Dino Books,
an imprint of John Blake Publishing,
The Plaza,
535 Kings Road,
Chelsea Harbour,
London SW10 0SZ

www.johnblakepublishing.com

www.facebook.com/johnblakebooks
twitter.com/jblakebooks

First published in paperback in 2019

ISBN: 978 1 78946 095 7

British Library Cataloguing-in-Publication Data:

A catalogue record for this book is available from the British Library.

Design by www.envydesign.co.uk

Printed and bound in Great Britain by Clays Ltd, Elcograf S.p.A.

1 3 5 7 9 10 8 6 4 2

Every reasonable effort has been made to trace copyright-holders of material reproduced in
this book, but if any have been inadvertently overlooked the publishers would be glad to
hear from them.

John Blake Publishing is an imprint of Bonnier Books UK
www.bonnierbooks.co.uk

For Sam Hughes – we listened!

Matt Oldfield is an accomplished writer and the editor-in-chief of football review site *Of Pitch & Page*. Tom Oldfield is a freelance sports writer and the author of biographies on Cristiano Ronaldo, Arsène Wenger and Rafael Nadal.

Cover illustration by Dan Leydon.
To learn more about Dan visit danleydon.com
To purchase his artwork visit etsy.com/shop/footynews
Or just follow him on Twitter @danleydon

CONTENTS

CHAPTER 1

THE GREAT WALL

13 January 2019, Wembley Stadium

As they waited in the tunnel, many of the Manchester United players were too excited to stand still. Star striker Marcus Rashford jumped up and down, midfield general Ander Herrera shook out his arms and legs, and captain Ashley Young clapped and cheered.

'This is it, lads – let's get stuck in straight away!'

David, however, stayed as calm and composed as ever. What was there to worry about? If his teammates needed him, United's Number One keeper would be there to save the day.

It had been a bad start to the Premier League
season, both for David and his football club.
However, things were starting to look a lot brighter.
Under new manager Ole Gunnar Solskjær, United
had won six games out of six. They had their
confidence back, but this would be their first big test
– Tottenham away.

For David, that meant the tough task of stopping
Harry Kane, one of the sharpest shooters in the
world. Kane wasn't Tottenham's only amazing
attacker either – they also had Son Heung-min, and
Dele Alli, and Christian Eriksen.

David, however, was determined. Despite a
difficult 2018 World Cup, he was still one of the
greatest goalkeepers in the world. It was time to
prove it. At his best, he was absolutely unbeatable!

'And I'm back to my best now,' he told himself
confidently, as the match kicked off.

In the first half, David didn't have very much to
do. Instead, United were up at the other end of the
pitch, attacking. Paul Pogba played a brilliant pass to
Rashford and he scored past Hugo Lloris. *1–0!*

'Yes!' David yelled, throwing his arms up in the air.

Right, time to really focus. He was about to become a very busy keeper. United were winning at Wembley, and it was David's job to keep it that way.

Kane fired a shot towards the far corner, but he stretched out his long right leg. SAVE!

David loved showing off his fantastic footwork. It was something that he had worked hard on with his first United goalkeeping coach, Eric Steele. Now, it was his superpower, his most dangerous weapon – but by no means his only weapon. When Alli steered a header towards the bottom corner, he dived down and stretched out his long arms just in time. SAVE!

'Who was marking him?' David wondered, but he didn't say it out loud – he wasn't a shouter like his United hero, Peter Schmeichel. Instead, he just got up and prepared himself for his next performance...

Alli burst through the United defence, but David stood up big and tall to block the shot. SAVE!

The Tottenham players couldn't believe it. Was there an invisible wall in front of the goal? No, it was just David, United's Great Wall.

Tottenham had chance after chance, but David made save after save.

Toby Alderweireld kicked the ball early on the volley, but David stretched out his long left leg. SAVE!

Kane's fierce free kick was curling in, but David flew through the air like superman. SAVE!

Not only did David keep the ball out, he managed to catch the ball too! 'Nice one!' the United centre-back Phil Jones said, giving his great goalkeeper a hug.

Tottenham weren't giving up yet, though. Alli got the ball in the penalty area again – would he be third time lucky? No, there was just no way past David. ANOTHER SAVE!

David never let his focus slip, not even for a second. Kane took another shot, but David stretched out his long right leg so far that he did the splits! SAVE!

'Are you okay?' Phil asked him, looking worried. 'That looked painful!'

David nodded calmly. He was fine – no big deal! In the last minute of the game, Érik Lamela swung a corner into the box, and David rushed out bravely to punch the ball downfield. It was the perfect way to end a perfect display.

As soon as the final whistle blew, David was surrounded by his thankful teammates.

'What a hero!' Ashley screamed in his face.

'We could have played another ninety minutes and they still wouldn't have scored!' Ander added.

'How many saves did you make?' Phil asked. 'I lost count ages ago!'

There were lots more happy hugs to come; with Ole, his manager; with Emilio Alvarez, his goalkeeping coach; and with his friend and teammate, Juan Mata.

Juan looked shocked, as if he'd just watched a magic show. 'I've never seen anything like it!' he said, with a huge smile on his face.

The United fans felt the same way. They clapped and clapped for their super keeper, singing his song over and over again:

He's big, he's brave, he's Spanish Dave,
He makes big saves, he never shaves,

He's flying through the air,
Come and have a shot if you dare!

Amongst those clapping along was Sir Alex
Ferguson, the old Manchester United manager
who had first brought him to England from Atlético
Madrid. Even during his early 'Dodgy Keeper!' days,
Sir Alex had been sure that David would one day go
on to become one of the best in the world.

José de Gea had always believed in his son too.
David had suffered setbacks along the way, but he
had bounced back every time. That resilience was
a crucial part of being a great goalkeeper. José knew
that from experience. Yes, he was a very, very proud
dad indeed.

CHAPTER 2

LIKE FATHER, LIKE SON

'Go on, son, take your best shot!' José called out, clapping his goalkeeper gloves together. 'I'm ready!'

Football was the De Gea family's favourite sport – so much so that José had even set up a mini-goal in their living room.

'It's not for me,' he promised his wife, Marivi. 'It's for David! I just want to give him the best possible start in life.'

It certainly seemed to be working. David fixed his eyes on the ball in front of him, with a look of real concentration on his little face. He was ready too – ready to score a great goal against his dad. As he ran forward, he pulled back his leg and kicked with all his might. *BANG!*

'What a shot!' José shouted out proudly as the ball flew towards him. It was a clean strike, with plenty of power. At the age of three, David already had a real rocket of a right foot. 'Like father like son,' José thought to himself happily. Of course, he let the ball roll under his diving body and into the back of the net.

'Noooooooooooooo!' José pretended to cry, slapping the carpet.

'GOOOOOOOOOOOOOOOAAAAAAAAAAAAAAAA AALLLLLLLLLLLLLLLLLL!' David screamed, running around the living room in circles, before jumping up and down on the sofa.

'Right – what next?' José asked, when his son had finally calmed down again. 'Do you want to take a few more shots?'

David shook his head.

'Okay, have you had enough for today?'

David shook his head again.

'My turn!' he said with a big smile.

His dad smiled too. 'What, you want to go in goal, eh? Like father, like son!'

José had been a professional keeper for Elche and Getafe, two football clubs who played in Spain's lower leagues. He had higher hopes for his son, however – David was going to play for the De Gea family's favourite football team, Atlético Madrid.

David had been born in Spain's capital city, but soon afterwards, the family moved away to a nearby town called Illescas. Still, he had already learned to cheer 'Atleti!' whenever he saw the red and white stripes on TV.

'Here you go,' José said, taking off his gloves and giving them to his son, but there was just one problem. When David put them on, they looked more like oven gloves than goalkeeper gloves on his tiny hands! No, he wouldn't be able to save anything with those on.

'Ha ha, maybe those will fit you in a few years!' José laughed. 'But for now...'

He rushed out of the room and returned with something hidden behind his back.

'...what do you think of these?'

David's eyes lit up – his own brand-new pair of kids' gloves! They were still a little big for him, but it was much better than wearing his dad's oven gloves.

'Right, are you ready?' José asked, placing the mini-ball on the mini-penalty spot.

David clapped his new gloves together, copying his dad exactly. 'GO!'

As the ball flew towards him, he watched it carefully, stretched out his right hand and...

'What a save!' his dad shouted out proudly. Whether he was scoring goals or stopping goals, David was a football natural.

'Like father, like son,' José thought to himself happily.

CHAPTER 3

FUTSAL STAR

Scoring goals or stopping goals? That was David's big decision. It was a really difficult choice to make because he was brilliant at both.

At his first school, *Colegio Castilla*, David chose to focus on scoring. Being the star striker was just more fun, especially when he was playing with his friends. Every day, he raced through the school gates, threw his bag down, and started the morning match.

'Let's go, we haven't got long before the bell!'

If David wasn't in class, he was almost always outside playing sport. He loved basketball and tennis too, but football was his favourite thing to do. Sometimes, they did keepy-uppies or headers and volleys in the playground, and other times, they played futsal – five-a-side indoor football – in the sports hall.

It didn't take the school team coach, José María Cruz, long to notice David's talent. In the passing and shooting drills, most of the youngsters just tried to kick the ball as hard as they possibly could. Their wild shots went everywhere, but usually high and wide.

'Don't forget to aim for the target!' Cruz got bored of telling them.

But there was one tall, skinny boy who already had the right idea. When the goal was there in front of him, he kept his cool and placed his shot right in the bottom corner.

'Fantastic finish! What's your name?' Cruz asked the blond-haired boy.

'David,' he replied.

'Well, David, congratulations! You're going to be our new striker.'

'Great!' he thought to himself. As much as David enjoyed playing in goal at home with his dad, it seemed like strikers got a lot more glory. Take his favourite team, Atleti, for example. Their keeper, José Francisco Molina, was so good that he also played in goal for the Spanish national team, but he was still nowhere near as famous as the club's new Number 9, Christian Vieri.

The message of that story? Everyone loves the guy who gets the goals! So, like most six-year-olds, David decided that he wanted to be Vieri, rather than Molina. In no time at all, he was the top scorer for the *Colegio Castilla* futsal team.

Dani slid the ball through to him and... *GOAL!*

David played a one-two with Juan and... *GOAL!*

Opposition defenders tried to stop David, with a tough tackle or a big push, but... *GOAL!*

'I reckon we could blindfold you, and you'd still score every time!' Cruz joked.

David wasn't just a fantastic finisher, though. As he grew older, he kept improving as an all-round footballer. He had the style of futsal to thank for that. The pitch was much smaller, and the ball was much heavier, so a defender couldn't just hoof it all the way up the field to the striker! No, futsal was all about touch and technique. To be a top player, you had to be able to pass and dribble your way out of small spaces, even as a striker.

'Check this out!' David announced to his teammates. He was about to try out a cool new trick in training. Carlos and Juan had boxed him in by the corner flag, but with a stepover, then a drag-back and then a backheel, he escaped with the ball. *GOAL!*

'Skillz!' Dani clapped and cheered.

David was well on his way to becoming a top futsal player, and that made José a very, very proud dad indeed. He was there at every match, cheering his son on. Although he was a striker at the moment, José still hoped that David might one day carry on the family tradition.

'Did you know that Pepe Reina started out as an attacker, just like you?' José told his son as they drove home from a game one day. He was trying to sound as casual as possible, but that name had certainly grabbed David's attention.

'Really?' he replied excitedly. Reina had just become Barcelona's new star goalkeeper.

'Yes, the best goalkeepers are always brilliant all-round footballers. You have to have skilful feet, as well as safe hands!'

'Cool, thanks, Dad!'

Marivi was a very proud mum too, but sometimes she worried that David was spending too much time running around with a ball at his feet, and not enough time sitting down doing his homework.

'Education is important!' she warned him again and again. 'If you don't study hard, you'll regret it one day.'

Just because his dad had become a professional footballer, that didn't mean that David would become one too. These things didn't just run in the family. He would need to have amazing talent, the right attitude, and good fortune as well. Marivi wanted her son to have a Plan B, just in case.

'How is David doing?' she often called up to ask his teachers. 'Is he paying attention in class? Does he seem tired? That boy plays so much sport, but school must come first.'

'Don't worry,' they always reassured her. 'David is doing just fine!'

CHAPTER 4

THE POPLAR AND THE GREAT DANE

At *Colegio Castilla*, David continued to be a star futsal striker. Outside of school, however, he decided to follow in his father's footsteps instead.

'Are you sure?' José asked him. The last thing he wanted to do was force his son to play a position that he hated.

But David just nodded. He was happy because putting on the goalkeeper gloves felt so familiar to him. It was like returning home, and it made sense for so many reasons:

1) He was tall for his age,
2) He was always calm,

3) He had really good reflexes for saving shots,
4) When he dived, he could fly through the air like superman,
And most importantly of all,
5) His dad was a goalkeeper too!

José was always there to give David lessons, whenever he wanted. There was nothing he liked more than talking about football. Every day was a school day in the De Gea house.

'Son, have I ever told you about "The Poplar"?' José asked David one afternoon.

He looked confused. 'No, what's that?'

'Well, a poplar is a tree, but it was also what they used to call José Ángel Iribar, my favourite goalkeeper of all time.'

'Why did they call him that?'

'Because when he came out to catch the ball, he jumped up tall and straight, just like a tree.'

'Did "The Poplar" play for Spain?' David asked.

'Yes, lots of times! He even played at the World Cup in 1966.'

'Cool! And did he play for Atleti too?'

'No, sadly not. He's from the Basque country, and so he chose to spend his whole career at Athletic Bilbao.'

'But why do you like him so much, Dad? What was so special about him?'

'I think it's easier if I just show you instead,' José said, searching for footage on the Internet. 'A-ha, found it! Here, let's watch this.'

Some of the video footage was so old that it was in black and white! But David didn't mind that; for him, watching 'The Poplar' in goal was like watching the most exciting action movie ever.

Iribar throwing himself down bravely at the feet of a striker,

Iribar jumping high to catch a cross.

'Hey, he's not even wearing gloves in that one!' David pointed out to his dad.

Iribar punching the ball out of the box,

Iribar tipping a free kick over the crossbar.

David's eyes stayed fixed on the computer screen, even after the video had ended.

'So, what did you think?' José asked eventually.

'I think he's... AMAZING!' David replied, his voice full of awe.

'Correct answer!' his dad laughed. 'Did you notice how quickly he moved across his goal? Incredible! They should have called him "The Panther", not "The Poplar"! But do you know what he was best at?'

'Catching?'

José shook his head.

'Kicking?'

José shook his head again.

'Concentrating! Being a goalkeeper can be a boring job at times. If your team is off attacking at the other end of the pitch, you don't have much to do. Some keepers switch off and lose their focus, but not Iribar. Never! "The Poplar" was always alert, always ready to save the day.'

In Iribar, David had his second goalkeeping hero (his first being his dad, of course!), and by the age of nine, he had his third.

David and José watched lots and lots of football together on TV – all the Atleti games, but also lots of

Champions League matches. For a young boy, it was so exciting to see so many excellent teams from all over Europe: Juventus from Italy, Dynamo Kyiv from Ukraine, Bayern Munich from Germany, and, best of all, Manchester United from England.

They were David's new favourite team. Sir Alex Ferguson's team had it all –

Ole Gunnar Solskjær's shooting,

Teddy Sheringham's heading,

Ryan Giggs's dribbling,

David Beckham's crossing,

Paul Scholes's passing,

Roy Keane's tackling,

and, best of all,

Peter Schmeichel's shotstopping.

David had never seen a goalkeeper like Schmeichel before. His nickname was 'The Great Dane', partly because he was from Denmark, but also partly because he was big and loved to bark, just like the dog.

'If I was a United defender, I'd be terrified of him!' José joked.

But there was a lot more to Schmeichel than just his shouting. He could make all kinds of super saves and when he jumped up in front of a striker, he pretty much blocked the whole goal!

It was 26 May 1999: Manchester United vs Bayern Munich at the Nou Camp in Barcelona. That Champions League Final was a night that David would never forget. It started with Schmeichel walking out on to the pitch as United captain, wearing his bright green goalkeeper shirt.

'Come on, Schmeichel!' David cheered, watching the game on TV in Spain.

And it ended with Solskjær scoring the winning goal in the very last minute of the match.

'Manchester! Manchester!' David shouted at the TV screen.

It hadn't been a busy night for 'The Great Dane', but he had still made two top saves to keep United in the game. Sheringham and Solskjær got the glory, but Schmeichel was the hero in David's eyes.

A few weeks later at school, the teacher asked the class to write down their plans for the future.

David's answer was short and sweet:

'I want to be like Peter Schmeichel.'

Yes, David dreamed of playing in goal for Manchester United, and winning the Champions League.

CHAPTER 5

CASARRUBUELOS

But how was David going to make his Manchester United dream come true? By working hard and listening to his coaches, that's how. Thankfully, he had two excellent people helping him.

First, there was his dad. José didn't just watch all of David's matches; he watched most of his training sessions too. Even in the freezing winter, with the rain lashing down on his umbrella, José was there, watching carefully. He was always honest with his son. If David played a blinder, he told him so. And if he had a stinker, he still told him so.

'Don't worry, there's always next week to put things right,' José liked to say. 'Learning from your mistakes is an important part of becoming a great goalkeeper.'

And then there was David's coach at Casarrubuelos, Juan Luis Martín. Casarrubuelos were a local youth club who were linked with David's favourite football team, Atlético Madrid. He even got to wear their badge proudly on his goalkeeper shirt.

'One day, you're going to be Atleti's Number One!' Martín wisely predicted.

The Casarrubuelos coach could see straight away that David had a very special talent. He was tall but also very agile, and he didn't mind diving across his goal, even on hard, dry pitches. In fact, he seemed to love it. And not only was he safe with his hands, but he was also skilful with his feet.

Yes, David was a very promising player indeed, but he needed to keep challenging himself in order to reach the top level. So each week, Martín came up with new tests for his young goalkeeper to complete.

'Right, you've got to catch thirty crosses in a row,' he said.

Easy! David had watched 'The Poplar' a million times, after all.

'Okay, I want to see you make ten saves to your left, then ten to your right.'

Easy! Thanks to José's coaching, he was strong on both sides.

David passed every test with flying colours – saving penalties, saving free kicks, saving one-on-ones, throwing, kicking, concentrating...

In the end, Martín could only smile and accept defeat. 'Fine, I guess you're just a natural, then!'

David's teammates definitely agreed. They loved having him there between the posts. The defenders didn't have to worry so much about making mistakes when they had the best goalkeeper in the league behind them.

The opposition striker was through on goal, with just David to beat... *BLOCK!*

A shot flew like an arrow towards the top corner of David's goal... *SAVE!*

The rebound fell to the striker, but David bounced back up... *DOUBLE SAVE!*

'Sorry!' his defenders panted as they chased back into position, but David never shouted at them like Schmeichel would have done. He preferred to stay calm and composed. Besides, he was just doing his job, after all.

'Please don't ever leave us,' Javier the centre-back begged. 'We'd fall apart without you!'

David enjoyed being the Casarrubuelos hero, but he had his heart set on bigger things: Atleti, Manchester United, Spain…

As he cheered his country on at the 2002 World Cup, David tried to imagine what it would feel like to be Iker Casillas. But that was impossible! At the age of only twenty-one, Casillas was already the Number One goalkeeper for Real Madrid *and* Spain.

'You can be that good,' José told his son confidently, 'if not even better.'

Really? David could see from his dad's face that he meant it. As good as Casillas? He was incredible, a super-keeper!

No, David couldn't think like that. He had to be confident and believe in himself. Otherwise, how would he ever go on and achieve his dreams?

'I can be that good,' he told his reflection in the mirror.

In his mind, David pictured a future Madrid Derby. The Vicente Calderón Stadium was like a bubbling cauldron of noise as the two teams walked out onto the pitch and took up their positions. In goal for Real, Iker Casillas. And in goal for Atleti... David de Gea!

CHAPTER 6

CATCHING ATLETI'S ATTENTION

If David kept saving the day for Casarrubuelos, surely an Atleti scout would eventually notice and sign him up. That was the plan, but what if that never happened?

'Just be patient,' José reassured him. 'You're twelve, not twenty-one!'

David tried to follow his dad's advice as usual, but patience wasn't easy. He had done his research on the Internet: Casillas had joined the Real Madrid youth academy at the age of nine, and he had been called up to the senior squad at the age of sixteen. For David, that was only four years away!

As he warmed up before each match, he looked around the edge of the pitch, searching for unfamiliar faces in the crowd, trying to identify a possible football scout. But who could it be? The old man wearing a hat? The woman under the umbrella? The young man walking his dog?

One person who did know the answer to that question was Martín, the Casarrubuelos coach. He was always on the lookout for scouts, just like David. He really didn't want to lose his star keeper, but at the same time, he didn't want to hold him back from reaching his full potential. David had the talent to go on and play for the Atleti first team; he was sure of it.

So, when one day an Atlético youth coach asked him if he had any good young goalkeepers, Martín mentioned David's name straight away.

'You're in luck, Emilio. I've got just the kid you're looking for!'

Martín talked the coach through David's many talents – the super saves, the brave blocks, the long throws, the accurate kicks.

'Why don't you come and watch him play next week? Trust me, you'll like him! The boy's dad will be there, and you can have a chat with him.

Remember José de Gea? He used to play in goal for
Getafe in the eighties.'

'Yeah, that name rings a bell,' Emilio García
replied. 'Thanks Juan, we'll check this kid out.'

Weeks passed, however, and there was no sign
of the Atleti youth coach. Martín hadn't heard from
him, and neither had David and José. Had García
simply found a better young keeper somewhere else?
Or was he just taking a very long time?

'Don't worry, I'll give him a call and find out
what's going on,' Martín reassured his young keeper.

Was there anything more that the Casarrubuelos
coach could do to help David? After a lot of thought,
he came up with a clever plan.

'Emilio, are you still looking for a young keeper?'
Martín asked on the phone.

'Yes, sorry, I've just been so busy recently,' Emilio
García explained.

'No problem, but I just thought I'd let you know
that Rayo Vallecano are ready to make David an offer.
So, if you're interested, you need to come down here
quick.'

Yes, it was a lie, but it was only a little white lie!
What harm could it possibly do?

There were a few seconds of silence as García
decided what to do next. 'Okay Juan, I'm sending
someone to watch your game this weekend.'

'Great, I'll let the boy's family know,' Martín said,
smiling to himself. His clever plan had worked perfectly!

García didn't just send any old scout to watch
David play; he sent Diego Díaz Garrido, a goalkeeper
who had played over sixty games for Atlético Madrid.

David recognised him as soon as he arrived at the
Casarrubuelos ground. *GULP!* This was it, the big
opportunity. Now the pressure was really on.

'Try not to think about it,' José told him before
kick-off. 'Just go out there and play your normal
game. Show him what you can do!'

David nodded and clapped his gloves together, just
like his dad used to do.

Fortunately, he didn't have to wait long to be
called into action. First, he made a good save to tip a
shot past the post, and then he came out to catch the
corner kick.

'Great work, David!' Martín cheered on the sidelines. He took a quick glance over at the Atlético scout. Surely, he was impressed?

He was. Diego had seen lots of young keepers who were good at some things, and not so good at other things. They all had weaknesses – but not this kid at Casarrubuelos.

David had the height, the reflexes, the bravery, the composure, *and* the understanding of the game. He was brilliant at saving, catching, throwing *and* kicking.

Yes, this David de Gea was the real deal, the complete package. There was no question about it. The opposition strikers had absolutely no chance of scoring past him.

As soon as the referee blew the half-time whistle, Diego was on the phone to García.

'So, what do you think?' the Atleti youth coach asked.

His reply was short and simple. 'Sign him straight away.'

CHAPTER 7

LIFE AT *LA CANTERA*

When he heard the news, David jumped for joy. His lifelong wish was about to come true. The De Gea family's favourite football team, Atlético Madrid, wanted to sign him.

'I did it, Dad!' David screamed. 'I did it!'

José wiped away his tears of pride and laughed heartily. 'My son, the Atleti star!'

David wasn't there yet, though. He still had a long way to go before his Madrid Derby dream became a reality, before he was competing against Casillas.

That was clear as soon as he arrived at *La Cantera*, the home of the club's youth academy. David just sat there staring out of the car window, with his mouth wide open. Wow, what a beautiful sight! There were hundreds of happy kids practising their football skills on perfect green pitches, with Spanish hills rising up in the distance.

As David watched them all warming up, suddenly the nerves set in. Atlético was going to be a big step-up from Casarrubuelos. What if he wasn't good enough? What if he made a total fool of himself? What if he couldn't save any of the strikers' shots?

With each doubt that entered his head, David's panic grew. Thankfully, his mum was there by his side to calm him down.

'Go on, you've got nothing to fear,' Marivi told him gently. 'Just enjoy yourself!'

David nodded, opened the car door and walked bravely into *La Cantera*.

García was there to welcome him and introduce him to the other Atlético Under-14 players. As he did, David just stood there, smiling shyly at all the unfamiliar faces. Being the new kid was rubbish!

One thing that David noticed straight away was the size of his teammates. He was one of the

tallest, but he was also the skinniest. Some of the
big boys could have snapped him like a little twig.
And, judging by the evil glares, the other goalkeeper
wanted to do just that!

GULP! It was a mighty relief when the training
session started. After a bit of catching practice, David
was put in goal for a shooting drill.

'Right, time to shine,' he muttered to himself.

He took a long, deep breath and danced from
foot to foot. He was ready to fly through the sky like
Superman. He was going to do everything possible to
keep this ball out of the net. He needed to make an
incredible first impression.

The striker played a one-two and ran on to the
return pass. As he pulled his leg back to shoot, David
searched for clues.

Which foot would he use? Right.

Which side of the goal would the striker aim for?
He was looking low to David's left.

Would he go for power or accuracy? Unfortunately,
David wouldn't really know that until the very last
second.

BANG! The striker curled the ball towards the bottom corner. David sprang across his goal, stretching out his long left arm as far as it would go... *SAVE!*

'Nice one, keeper!' his new coach clapped and cheered.

David was delighted but he didn't show any emotion. He just picked himself up off the grass and prepared to save the next shot too.

'So, how did it go?' his mum asked on the long journey back to Illescas.

David shrugged. 'Okay, thanks.'

Marivi was used to her son's short replies; he was a teenager now. 'And?' she added.

'The coach says I'll be starting in goal for the match on Sunday.'

'That's my boy!' she cried out. 'Congratulations, I knew you could do it!'

It turned out that playing for Atleti was exactly the challenge that David needed. He thrived under the pressure, making supersave after supersave against the best young strikers in Spain.

'Man, how did we cope before you came along?' the left-back Álvaro Domínguez wondered.

David smiled and shrugged. What could he say? First Casarrubuelos and now Atleti; he just loved being the hero!

'What did I tell you?' his dad said with a smirk. 'My son, the Atleti star!'

Even though *La Cantera* was a long way from Illescas, José hardly missed a minute of David's performances. He didn't just watch all of his son's matches; he watched most of his training sessions too. Even during the freezing winter, with the rain lashing down on his umbrella, José was there, watching carefully.

And even though Atlético had some of the top goalkeeper trainers in the country, David still always listened to his dad's advice. José had been his first coach and he would always be his most important. So he would always reply: 'Yes, Dad!' or 'Thanks, Dad!'

But just when David felt like he had conquered *La Cantera*, a new challenge came his way. Suddenly, he wasn't the only talented young keeper at Atleti.

Joel Robles was the same age as David, and even taller. He was also already a Spanish Under-16 international.

'You need to show this new guy who's boss!' Domínguez told him, but that wasn't David's style. He wasn't a shouter like Schmeichel. He would let his saves do the talking.

Off the pitch, David and Joel became good friends. On the pitch, however, they became fierce rivals, fighting to be Atleti's future Number One. The battle helped to bring out the best in both of them.

'That spot is *mine!*' David told himself after pulling off yet another wondersave.

No, David wasn't the loudest, but he was the most determined. Anything Joel could do, he could do too. Soon, David was off on an international adventure of his own.

CHAPTER 8

2007: A SPECIAL SPANISH SUMMER

'Come on, we can win this!' David told his Spanish teammates confidently as they set off for Belgium to play in the UEFA European Under-17 Championship.

He couldn't wait to represent his country in a proper, major tournament. What a proud moment it would be! So far, everything was going according to his football dreams. First the Spain Under-15s, and now the Under-17s. He was following in the glove-prints of his goalkeeper heroes like José 'The Poplar' Iribar and Iker Casillas.

Viva España!

After twenty-four years of disappointment, at last the future of the Spanish national team looked bright again. Now, they had a senior squad full of superstars like Xavi, Casillas, Andrés Iniesta and David Villa. '*La Roja*' could beat anyone, and so could their Under-17s.

The core of Spain's youth team was incredible: Barcelona's Bojan in attack, Arsenal's Fran Mérida in midfield, Real Madrid's Nacho in defence and, of course, David in goal! He was wearing Number 13, rather than Number 1, but there was no doubt that he was the first-choice stopper.

'Yes, we've got the talent,' their coach Juan Santisteban told them, 'but have we got the winning mentality? If we're not focused, we'll fail!'

David was always focused. That was one of the many things that made him such a clever keeper. Neither France nor Germany could score past him.

'Yes, that's two clean sheets already!' David cheered, high-fiving Nacho. To them, they were almost as important as goals.

Spain were through to the semi-finals! Next

up were Belgium and their deadly attacking duo,
Christian Benteke and Eden Hazard. David made
some super saves but there was nothing he could do
when Hazard's shot deflected off Spain's defender,
David Rochela.

'Noooo!' David's heart sank. He really hated letting
in goals.

But luckily, Bojan equalised and, after extra time,
the semi-final went to penalties. As a goalkeeper,
this was David's time to shine. He could become a
national hero!

As the first Belgian player placed the ball down on
the spot, David took a long, deep breath and threw
his long arms out, high and wide. He was ready to fly
through the sky like Superman.

But De Pauw scored,

and so did Spruyt,

and so did Zevne,

and so did Hazard...

Aquino didn't score, but he blazed over the bar.
After seven penalties each, David still hadn't made a
single save.

'Come on!' he told himself. 'Stop this next one, and we're in the final!'

He looked up and saw his teammates on the halfway line, cheering him on. They were counting on him.

Belgium's captain Dimitri Daeseleire stepped up and… SAVE!

David got back to his feet and punched the air with both fists. He had done it – he was Spain's spot-kick hero! Seconds later, he was at the bottom of a big pile of grateful players.

'Thanks, what a save!'

'You're a legend!'

Viva España!

In the UEFA European Under-17 Championship Final, it was Spain vs England. Could David and co. keep a third clean sheet?

When Bojan scored early in the second half, David threw his arms up in the air. However, he didn't let his focus slip. The match was still far from over.

With half an hour to go, England fired a fizzing free kick towards the bottom corner. The Spain defenders turned, fearing the worst, but David dived down and stretched out his long left arm as far as it would go… *SAVE!*

David was delighted but he didn't show it. He just pulled up his socks and got ready for the corner-kick.

When the referee blew the final whistle, the Spain players ran towards each other and bounced up and down together. David was one of the last to join the happy huddle. On the sideline, their coaches were doing the same thing.

What an achievement – Spain were the Champions of Europe! And that meant their international adventure was only just beginning. In August, David and his teammates travelled to South Korea to challenge for the FIFA Under-17 World Cup trophy.

'Right, let's keep this run going!' Santisteban urged his players and they listened.

Spain 4 Honduras 2
Spain 2 Syria 1
Spain 1 Argentina 1

David was disappointed that he hadn't kept any

clean sheets yet, but there was still time for that. Spain were through to the next round.

Against North Korea, David didn't have much to do, but he never let his focus slip.

'Concentrate!' he kept telling himself. 'At some point, your team will need you.'

David was right. A shot deflected off a Spanish defender and changed direction completely. Suddenly, the ball was curling into the bottom corner... no, SAVE!

What a stop! David certainly deserved his first clean sheet of the tournament. 'Quarter-finals, here we come!' he cheered at the final whistle.

Spain had beaten France 2–0 at the Euros, but it was a much more competitive match at the World Cup. After 120 minutes, the score was still 1–1. Time for penalties! As a goalkeeper, it was David's time to shine once more.

'We believe in you!' Bojan said, giving him a big hug. 'We need you to be our spot-kick hero again!'

But Sakho scored,
and so did Le Tallec. *2–2!*

'I should have got my glove to that one!' David moaned. But there was no time for self-criticism, he had to keep focus and keep believing in himself. He clapped his gloves together and prepared for the next penalty. 'All I have to do is make one save, and we're in the semi-finals!'

Thibault Bourgeois stepped up and... SAVE!

'Yes!' David roared like a lion.

Thanks to their super-keeper, Spain now had the advantage.

Bojan scored,

and so did Fran,

and so did Dani Aquino. They were the winners!

'Next time, can we just win in normal time please?' David teased his relieved teammates.

Spain didn't beat Ghana in ninety minutes, but they did beat them in 120. Just when another penalty shoot-out was looming, Bojan scored the winning goal. *Phew!*

David's dream had come true. He was about to play in a World Cup Final – Spain vs Nigeria.

As the two teams walked out onto the pitch, it

really felt like a final. The stadium was filled with over 36,000 fans. That meant four times more noise than in the semis!

During the national anthems, David soaked up the amazing atmosphere around him. But as soon as the music stopped, he was fully focused on winning another trophy. Spain were the favourites, but that meant nothing now.

'Let's do this!' David cheered.

But as hard as they tried, neither team could score. First, Spain had a shot cleared off the line.

'Ohhhhhhhh!' David groaned with his hands on his head.

Then, Nigeria's left winger cut inside and went for goal. It was a powerful strike, but not powerful enough to get past David. He sprang up and tipped the ball over the bar.

'Thanks, superman!' Nacho said, patting him on the back.

The game was goalless after 90 minutes, and it was still goalless after 120 minutes too. It was time for one last penalty shoot-out.

David was desperate to be Spain's spot-kick hero in the World Cup final. Sadly, however, it wasn't to be this time.

Nigeria scored three penalties out of three, while Spain didn't score a single one. 3–0! It was all over in a flash and Nigeria's keeper, Dele Ajiboye, was the spot-kick hero. David's World Cup dream had been destroyed.

'Hey, there was nothing more you could have done,' Santisteban comforted his keeper. 'You were the best goalie in the whole tournament. This is just the start for you!'

David returned home with mixed feelings. It was very disappointing not to win the World Cup, but he was pleased with his performances. He had made a real name for himself during that special Spanish summer. What next?

CHAPTER 9

OUT ON LOAN OR TRAIN ALONE?

When he arrived back at Atlético, David still had a keeper battle to win. Yes, he was improving with every game, but so was Joel. David couldn't just sit back and relax after his achievements with Spain. If he wanted to become an Atleti star one day, he had to keep fighting.

Just like at the Under-17 World Cup, David rose to every challenge that faced him. He stayed fully focused and he didn't put a foot, or glove, wrong. With every super save and brave block, he was proving Diego right; he *was* the complete package, the real deal.

Ultimately, there could only be one winner. As the 2008–09 season loomed, the club made their crucial decision: Joel would play for Atlético Madrid C, and David would play for... Atlético Madrid B!

David had won the battle, and he had his first professional contract to prove it. He would be staying at his favourite football team until at least 2011.

'By then, I'll be the Number One!' he thought to himself.

One challenge completed – on to the next! This was going to be a big step-up for David, maybe even bigger than when he moved from Casarrubuelos to *La Cantera*.

Atlético B played in *Segunda División B*, the third level of the Spanish football league. For the first time, David wouldn't just be playing against his own age group. He was still only eighteen, but now he would be facing strikers who were twenty-five, or thirty, or maybe even thirty-five. Thirty-five? That was nearly twice his age!

'I know you're ready for this,' his dad told him. 'Just remember, get your body behind the ball!'

David wasn't worried. This was just the next step on his road to the top. Besides, Casillas had been even younger when he started his career at Real Madrid C.

Atlético B played thirty-eight league games that season, and David started thirty-five of them. That was more than any other player in the squad. With the team struggling near the bottom of the table, he had plenty of work to do.

David dived down low to keep out a stinging strike. SAVE!

David sprang up and stretched out his long left arm. SAVE!

David stuck out his long right leg to deflect a shot wide. SAVE!

He had already caught the eye of scouts during the Under-17 World Cup, but now he was doing it week-in, week-out for Atlético B. By the summer of 2009, most of Europe's top clubs were scouting him.

Juventus had Gianluigi Buffon for now, but what if he moved on?

Manchester United had Edwin van der Sar for now, but he was nearly at the end of his career. What would happen when he retired?

David would be the ideal replacement for the Dutchman. In Spain, they had even started calling him 'Van der Gea' because their styles were so similar. They were both very tall and skinny, with skilful feet and safe hands. And hadn't David always dreamed of playing for Manchester United?

The plan seemed perfect, but David couldn't leave Spain yet, not before becoming Atleti's Number One.

In Summer 2009, that shirt belonged to Sergio Asenjo, a young keeper who had just signed from Valladolid. And then there was the 'Number 13', Roberto. He was twenty-eight years old, with lots more experience.

'Let the battle begin!' David declared, but the Atlético Madrid Sporting Director disagreed. Jesús García Pitarch wanted his youngest keeper to go out on loan.

'It's the best way for you to keep developing your skills,' Pitarch argued. 'Trust me, you need game-time, not bench-time! I've got two great options for you: stay here in Spain with Numancia or go to England and play for QPR.'

David took some time to talk it through with his

parents. But the more he thought about it, the more he realised that he didn't like either option. What he wanted was to stay at Atlético and prove himself. He was only one year younger than Sergio, and surely, he was good enough to compete?

David wasn't the loudest character at the club, but he could be stubborn when he wanted to be. When he gave Pitarch his answer, the Sporting Director was very angry. 'Fine, well if you won't go out on loan, then you'll have to train alone!'

What? David couldn't believe it, and neither could his parents. It was so unfair! José was all ready to storm into Pitarch's office but Marivi managed to calm him down.

'Give it a few days,' she said. 'Hopefully, he'll change his mind.'

In the end, it worked out brilliantly for David because training alone helped him to stand out even more! One day, Atlético's first team coach, Abel Resino, noticed David doing some catching practice over in the corner of the field. He looked so lonely out there on his own.

'What's going on?' Resino muttered to himself. 'That kid is meant to be Atleti's next great keeper!'

Oh well, if the B team didn't want him, the A team could always use another pair of hands. With two keepers, there was rivalry, but with three, there would be real competition. That could only be a good thing for Atlético.

'Kid, come with me!' Resino shouted across the field.

David nodded eagerly and followed the manager over to where the first team was training. Wow, was this really happening? Yes, it was! David tried to play it as cool as possible, but his heart was thudding like a hammer in his chest.

'Dani, David is joining us today,' Resino called out to one of his coaches. 'I thought our strikers might need some extra shooting practice!'

A few weeks later, Wigan Athletic made a bid to buy David. Their new Spanish manager, Roberto Martínez, was a big fan of the young keeper.

'If you come here, I'll make you a Premier League star!' he promised.

'No thanks!' David replied and this time, Atlético said the same. They didn't want to sell him. Phew! Now he was all set to achieve his lifelong dream: becoming Atleti's Number One.

CHAPTER 10

ON FIRE IN THE FIRST TEAM

Yes, 2009–10 was going to be David's season; he was more determined than ever. However, training with the first team was both exciting and exhausting. This was the big time now. David couldn't switch off for a single second. If he did, the ball was in the back of his net before he even noticed.

'Wake up, David!' the goalkeeping coach shouted. 'You've got to get down quicker!'

It was a steep learning curve for an eighteen-year-old. The Atlético squad was packed with so many fantastic finishers.

When it came to long-range shots, wingers Maxi

Rodríguez and Simão Sabrosa could find the top corner with almost every kick. And they could hit the ball so hard! Even when David dived at full stretch, he often couldn't reach out his long arms in time.

'Unlucky, great effort!' the coach encouraged him.

And when it came to close-range shots, Atleti's two South American strikers were the best in the business. The previous season, Uruguayan Diego Forlán had scored the most goals in the entire Spanish league. And Argentinian Sergio Agüero was just as brilliant in the box, if not better. *BANG! GOAL!*

'How am I supposed to stop that?' David asked himself all the time.

He was definitely improving, though, and he was also making friends. He already knew Koke and Domínguez from the youth team, and he discovered that the older players weren't as scary as expected. In fact, they were very friendly.

'Hi, David!' a voice called out in the lunch canteen.

David turned around; it was Agüero. 'Oh, hi Sergio!'

'Call me Kun,' he replied. 'Everyone calls me Kun.'

'My new friend, Kun,' David thought to himself. 'How cool is that?'

Things were about to get even cooler. In September, Sergio Asenjo went away to play for Spain at the Under-20 World Cup. That meant that David was bumped up from third-choice to second-choice keeper. Now there was only Roberto ahead of him. David would be there on the bench for Atlético's next game – Barcelona at the Nou Camp!

'That's wonderful news, son,' José shouted down the phone. 'Congratulations, we'll be there watching!'

David didn't get to play and Atlético lost, but it was still an amazing experience for him. When Kun was substituted, he slumped down in the seat next to David.

'Don't worry, you'll be out there soon!' the Argentinian predicted. By the final whistle, Roberto had let in five goals.

The next week, David watched from the bench as Atlético drew 2–2 with Almería.

'You should be playing!' his dad argued passionately.

The week after that, David was on the bench
again, this time in Porto for Atleti's Champions
League match. Just when he was sitting comfortably,
he was suddenly called into action. After twenty-five
minutes, Roberto made a signal to the sidelines. He
was injured, and he couldn't carry on.

'David, get ready!' a coach shouted. 'You're
coming on!'

What a moment for David to make his Atleti
debut! In a flash, he jumped up, took off his
tracksuit, and pulled his gloves on. Right, it was his
time to shine.

As he jogged into his penalty area, the centre-back
Juanito came over. 'Good luck, you're going to be
great!'

'Thanks, mate!'

David placed the ball down carefully and sent a
long goal kick down the field towards Kun. So far, so
good.

At half-time, it was 0–0, and after seventy
minutes, it was still 0–0. David was enjoying himself
and he was putting on a goalkeeping masterclass.

He pushed a shot past the post. SAVE!

'Well done!' Juanito said, giving David a high-five.

He tipped a free kick over the bar. SAVE!

He came out to clear a cross away. PUNCH!

He bravely blocked a blast from Hulk. SAVE!

Could David keep a clean sheet on his Atleti debut? No, not quite. The ball bounced back to Hulk and he crossed to Radamel Falcao, who backheeled it in. 1–0 to Porto!

'Noooooooo!' David fell to the floor in disappointment. All of his hard work had gone to waste.

He didn't just give up, though. No, he wasn't done yet.

As Falcao headed the ball towards goal, he was sure that he would score... but no, David was there to block it: another SAVE!

'Come on!' David cried out, clapping his gloves together. He could shout like Schmeichel when he needed to.

But from the corner, Falcao hit the post and Rolando tapped in the rebound. 2–0 to Porto!

David was furious at the performance of his side's defence. What were they doing? He didn't care that he was only eighteen and that it was only his debut; he expected more from his teammates.

At the final whistle, David shook hands with the Porto players and then trudged off the pitch. Resino was waiting for him by the tunnel.

'Kid, you were incredible tonight,' the manager said, patting him on the back. 'You're going to be a superstar!'

Three days later, David made his home debut against Real Zaragoza. He wasn't a sub anymore; he was starting for Atleti at the Vicente Calderón! He had to pinch himself to check that it was real.

David's childhood dream nearly turned into a nightmare, however. After twenty minutes, a Zaragoza midfielder played a through ball into his penalty area. David had to do something, but he made the wrong decision. He raced out and fouled the striker. *Penalty!*

Uh oh, could David make up his mistake? He hoped so. He thought back to his saves for the Spain

Under-17s. He could do this.

As Marko Babić ran up, David didn't move. Then at the very last second, he dived down low to his left and... SAVE!

'What a stop!' his teammates ran over to tell him. 'You're a hero!'

David was delighted but he didn't show it. He just got on with the game.

In the second half, Zaragoza did score their second penalty but by then, Atlético had already won the match. At the final whistle, David wasn't ready to leave the field yet. He wanted his big night to go on and on. So, he walked all the way around the pitch, clapping the fans.

Wait, what were they singing? At first, David couldn't believe what he was hearing. The Atleti supporters were chanting his name!

De Gea! De Gea! De Gea!

CHAPTER 11

EL NIÑO WINS THE EUROPA LEAGUE

Despite David's amazing displays, Sergio Asenjo returned from the Under-20 World Cup and went straight back into the Atlético team, replacing David.

'Bring back De Gea!' the fans begged when they lost 3–0 to Osasuna.

There were moans and groans, and plenty of boos. Something had to change. At this point, Atleti were placed seventeenth in the Spanish league, only one point above the relegation zone.

'We finished fourth last season!' people complained.

By October 2009, Atlético had a new manager, Quique Sánchez Flores. And for David, that also meant a new goalkeeping coach.

'Think of this as a fresh start,' Emilio Álvarez announced at the first training session. 'It's time to shine, guys. I want to see what each of you can do.'

Sánchez Flores had asked him to take a look at all three of Atlético's stoppers:

1) Sergio Asenjo, the current Number One,
2) Roberto, the experienced back-up,
And 3) David, the kid, or '*El Niño*' as coaches called him.

'So, what did you think?' the manager asked when they met up in the afternoon.

Emilio had his answer ready. 'The best of the three is *El Niño.*'

Sánchez Flores nodded: 'Then he'll be our keeper.'

David still wore the 'Number 43' shirt, but before long, he was really Atlético's Number One. Even when he made costly errors, they stuck with him.

'These things happen,' Emilio explained, 'especially when you're a young goalie. What matters is how you learn from your mistakes.'

Wasn't that exactly what José had always told him? Emilio firmly believed that David would one day become one of the best keepers around. Just like David's old Casarrubuelos coach Martín, Emilio was always setting crazy new challenges for him to complete.

'Wait, why do I have to wear a blindfold?' David asked. He didn't like not being able to see anything. It was unsettling. 'You're not going to fire balls at me, are you?'

'Don't worry,' the goalkeeping coach replied, 'only from close range! It's to improve your reflexes. Right, are you ready? Go!'

With Emilio, every training session was exciting and different. David never knew what he was going to do next, but whatever it was, it always helped to make him a better keeper.

With David in goal, Atlético leapt back up the league table. Their recovery began when they beat Barcelona. At the Vicente Calderón, Diego and Simão put them 2–0 up after twenty-three minutes. While the fans went wild, their keeper kept calm.

'Stay focused!' David called out to his defenders, clapping his gloves together.

Zlatan Ibrahimović scored once, but he wasn't scoring twice. No way! David made sure of that, with save after save.

'What a win!' Kun cheered, hugging his heroic goalkeeper.

David was still just nineteen years old, but his teammates already trusted him. He was a winner and that's what Atleti needed.

The club had only won one trophy in the previous fourteen years, but that losing streak was about to end. Because with stars like David, Simão, Diego and Kun, the team now had the strength to succeed. Atlético finished ninth in La Liga, and they made it all the way to two big finals – the Europa League and the Spanish Cup.

'Surely, we've got to win at least one of them,' Juanito hoped.

Diego shook his head: 'That's not the right attitude. Come on, we're going to win BOTH!'

The Europa League final came first, in May 2010.

Atlético had already knocked out Liverpool in the semi-finals and now they were up against another English team – Fulham.

Forget the Under-17 World Cup final – this was David's new favourite football experience ever! As the teams walked out onto the pitch, they were greeted by the sounds of 49,000 supporters.

Fulham! Fulham!

Atleti! Atleti!

David had booked as many tickets as possible for his friends and family. They had all travelled out to Germany to – fingers crossed! – to see him lift his first senior trophy.

Would David be nervous on such a special occasion? Not a chance! When Simon Davies fired a shot at goal, he didn't just save it; he caught it!

In the crowd, José smiled to himself. 'Good, he's feeling confident!'

Diego put Atlético 1–0 up, but Davies equalised five minutes later. This time, David didn't have a chance.

'Keep going!' he urged his teammates on.

When the match went to extra time, David started

thinking about penalties. What a feeling it would be to become Atleti's Europa League hero! At least he had lots of shoot-out experience with Spain…

In the end, however, that wasn't needed. In the 116th minute, Kun sprinted down the left wing and crossed to Diego. With a clever flick, he scored the winner!

Watching from his penalty area, David punched the air, but he didn't join in the big celebrations. That could wait. The last minutes ticked by so slowly. *Four, three, two, one…* finally it was over – Atlético had won the Europa League!

As soon as the referee blew the final whistle, David was off, racing across the grass to hug his teammates.

'We did it!' he screamed.

Campeones, Campeones, Olé! Olé! Olé!

Even amid all the excitement, David still remembered to run over and thank Emilio. 'I really couldn't have done this without you!' he admitted, his voice full of emotion.

'Don't mention it,' the goalkeeping coach replied modestly. 'Go enjoy yourself – you deserve it!'

Once the Atleti players had picked up their winners' medals, it was time for captain Antonio López to lift the trophy.

'Hurray!' David shouted, throwing his arms up into the air. What a fantastic feeling!

After that, it was time to get the party started. They sang and danced and paraded the cup in front of their fans. At last, they had something to cheer about! When David spotted his friends and family, he gave them a big wave. It was so nice to share his special night with them. He knew how proud his parents would be.

Atleti couldn't get too carried away, though. They still had another final left to play. A week later, they faced Sevilla in the Spanish Cup.

Sadly, there would be no second success for Atlético. Sevilla scored twice and there was nothing that David could do to stop either goal.

Losing was a horrible feeling, especially in a final. But at least David had one winners' medal to show from his sensational first season. And he was already looking forward to the next.

CHAPTER 12

COMPLIMENTS FROM CASILLAS

Ahead of the 2010 World Cup in South Africa, the Spain manager Vicente del Bosque called together a group of the country's thirty best players. In that group there were five goalkeepers:

Casillas from Real Madrid,
Pepe Reina from Liverpool,
Víctor Valdés from Barcelona,
Diego López from Villareal...
And David de Gea from Atlético Madrid!

'Dad, I made it!' David told José happily. Was the

Atleti goalkeeper's debut season about to get *even* better?

Perhaps, but out of the thirty players at the training camp, only twenty-three would go to the World Cup. And of the five goalkeepers, Del Bosque would only take three. So, unless there was an injury, David knew that his chances were very, very low.

'Hey, don't worry about that,' Emilio told him as they said their goodbyes. 'You're still young. Just enjoy the experience!'

David did just that. At first, he felt shy around Spain's superstars, but he was eager to learn as much as possible from them. One minute, he was taking tips from Casillas and the next, he was testing himself against Fernando Torres.

'Great save!' the coaches clapped and cheered. David hoped that Del Bosque was paying attention too.

In the end, David didn't make it into the Spain squad, but he wasn't too disappointed. Hopefully, he would have plenty more World Cups ahead of him.

Back at Atlético, David stormed into the 2010–11

season like an express train. Now that he'd had a taste of glory, he wanted more: more saves, more clean sheets, and, most importantly, more trophies!

His first opportunity came in August 2010, the UEFA Super Cup final against the Champions League winners, Inter Milan. This time, Atlético were the underdogs, but their booming fans filled them with belief.

Atleti! Atleti! Atleti!

Their players were pumped up and ready to win. David was up against two of the sharpest shooters in the world: Samuel Eto'o and Diego Milito. Could he stop them from scoring?

David didn't have many saves to make, but he kept himself busy. He was always watching, moving, talking, and organising his defence.

'Mark up!'

'Domínguez, that's your man!'

Atlético were playing really well and in the second half, they took the lead. José Antonio Reyes dribbled through and scored past Júlio César. 1–0!

'Yes!' In his penalty area, David lept high into the

sky, punching the air in delight. 'Come on!'

With ten minutes to go, Simão crossed to Kun. He couldn't miss. 2–0!

David punched the air again. Was that game over? No, not quite. In the last minute, Raúl García fouled Goran Pandev in the box. *Penalty to Inter!*

No problem – David didn't panic. He wanted that clean sheet desperately. This was his time to shine.

As Milito moved towards the ball, David stayed still. Then at the very last second, he dived down low to his right and stretched his long left arm upwards... SAVE!

David jumped to his feet with a mighty roar. That's right, he was unbeatable! He was a spot-kick hero once again.

'You legend!' the Atleti right-back Tomáš Ujfaluši screamed, giving him a big hug.

A trophy *and* a clean sheet – what a start!

And David's success didn't stop there. Against Barcelona, he made a series of super saves to keep out shots from Xavi, Pedro, David Villa *and* Lionel Messi. Even though Atlético still lost 2–1, David was

MATT AND TOM OLDFIELD

still the man of the match without doubt.

'If it wasn't for you, it would have been 5–1, at least!' Kun admitted.

Three days later, David was at it again. Opponents Valencia attacked and attacked, but they just couldn't score past Atleti's amazing keeper.

A header from Aritz Aduriz... SAVE!

A shot from Juan Mata... SAVE!

Eventually, Valencia did score but Atleti held on for a draw.

David was on fire! Everyone was talking about his talent, including one of his all-time heroes – Iker Casillas. 'De Gea has been doing very well,' the Real Madrid goalkeeper told the newspapers. 'He reminds me a lot of when I started playing eleven years ago.'

When David read Casillas' comments, he couldn't believe it. What a compliment!

On 7 November 2010, the two goalkeepers finally met at opposite ends of the football field. It was the Madrid Derby, Real vs Atlético, just like David had dreamt it! But who would win the battle? Could David stop Cristiano Ronaldo from scoring?

Yes, he could, but unfortunately, Real Madrid had lots of other excellent players too. Ricardo Carvalho got the first goal and Mesut Özil got the second. 2–0!

There was nothing that David could do, except keep going. If Casillas could shine at the other end, then so could he.

Pepe headed the ball powerfully, but David jumped high and held on to it. SAVE!

Marcelo poked a shot goalwards, but David got down quickly. SAVE!

Ronaldo tried to trick him at his near post, but David wasn't fooled. SAVE!

Karim Benzema shot from the edge of the box, but he couldn't beat David. SAVE!

At the final whistle, the match ended 2–0 to Real, but their winning margin could have been wider still if it hadn't been for David.

'Well played,' Casillas said as the two goalkeepers hugged. 'You've got a new enemy now. Cristiano's furious that he didn't score today!'

And there was more praise to come. Del Bosque declared that David was 'the future of the Spanish national team'.

Wow, what a thing to hear! David beamed with pride. Everything was going so well for him.

As David's reputation grew and grew, Europe's biggest clubs fought harder and harder to buy him. David loved Atleti with all his heart, but would they ever be able to compete with clubs like Real Madrid and Manchester United?

It was a topic that David often talked about with his best friend Kun. When Atlético played away games, they shared a room together. While watching TV or playing PlayStation, they liked to chat. The Argentinian striker was thinking about the future too:

'I'm nearly twenty-three now and there's so much I still want to achieve. One day, I want to win the Champions League!'

David nodded. 'Yeah, me too!'

'I think it might be time for me to move to a bigger club. What about you – are you going to stay for another season?'

David shrugged. 'I'm not sure yet. Right now, I'm just focusing on the Euros.'

CHAPTER 13

EUROPEAN CHAMPIONS (AGAIN!)

Yes, David was off to Denmark to play in the 2011 UEFA European Under-21 Championships. He had won the Euros with the Spain Under-17s, but then failed with the Under-19s. What would happen this third time?

'We'll win it, of course!' Bojan boasted confidently.

Expectations were very high because Spain looked stronger than ever. They had César Azpilicueta in defence, Javi Martínez, Ander Herrera and Thiago Alcântara in midfield, and Juan Mata and Adrián in attack. Wow, with a squad like that, no wonder they were the favourites to win the trophy!

In their first game, against England, Spain took the lead early, thanks to Ander. So far so good – but in the last minutes of the match, England's Danny Welbeck equalised.

'That's what happens when you switch off!' Spain's coach, Luis Milla, told them angrily in the dressing room afterwards. For a few moments, David and his teammates just sat there, staring down at their dirty boots. The draw felt more like a defeat. But there was no point feeling sorry for themselves; they had to bounce back to winning ways.

In the next game, Ondřej Čelůstka headed the ball down towards David's bottom corner... SAVE! It finished Spain 2 Czech Republic 0.

In the game after that, Yevhen Konoplyanka took on David from the penalty spot... SAVE! It finished Spain 3 Ukraine 0.

'That's more like it!' Milla cheered happily. His team was through to the Euro semi-finals!

After those two wins in a row, the Spanish players were feeling confident again about the semi-final. A little *too* confident, actually. They passed and passed but they weren't creating any goalscoring chances. In goal, David grew more and more frustrated.

'Do they think they can just walk the ball into the net?' he muttered to himself.

Instead, it was Belarus who took the lead. From a long throw, Andrey Voronkov somehow pulled off an amazing overhead kick. David could only watch as the ball rolled off the post and over the goal-line. *1–0!*

What on earth had just happened? What were the defenders doing? David looked up at the sky for answers, but it didn't help. Spain had let Belarus score with their very first shot of the game.

'Come on, wake up!' David clapped and cheered.

Spain improved in the second half, but their strikers still couldn't find a way past the goalkeeper.

'Maybe I should go up front!' David thought to himself, remembering his glorious futsal days. He was still a fantastic finisher in training... But just as he started to creep forward out of his penalty area, Adrián finally scored for Spain. And after that, there was only going to be one winner: 2–1, 3–1... *phew*, what a relief!

After their scare against Belarus, Spain were fully

focused for the final. They had a trophy to lift.

Switzerland were a talented team, though, and very tough to beat. They had a strong defence and exciting attackers too. Their winger Xherdan Shaqiri hit a vicious volley, but David was ready for it. SAVE!

'Ow, I bet that hurt your hands!' Domínguez joked as they high-fived.

David just shrugged. He didn't mind a moment of pain, as long as they won the tournament.

After that, Spain took control of the game. Ander scored a header before half-time, and then Thiago made it two.

'Yes!' David cried out, jumping for joy. He was about to become a European Champion again.

At the final whistle, the Spanish players celebrated in style. They bounced up and down as a big band of brothers. Together, they had lived up to those very high expectations.

Campeones, Campeones, Olé! Olé! Olé!

Eventually, Javi, their captain, went up to collect the trophy. He kissed it lovingly and then lifted it high above his head.

'Hurray!' the other players cheered around him.

As the tallest in the team, David was stood at the back, behind Javi. He couldn't wait any longer. When no-one was looking, he reached up with his long right arm, until he was touching the trophy too!

Campeones, Campeones, Olé! Olé! Olé!

As Del Bosque had said, David was the future of the Spanish national team. He was still only twenty now, but in the years to come, he would become his nation's Number One. David would be the keeper to take over from Casillas, and he was now more determined than ever.

CHAPTER 14

MOVING TO MANCHESTER UNITED

Eric Steele had been admiring David for a very long time. In fact, the Manchester United goalkeeping coach had been a fan of his ever since he won the Under-17 Euros in 2007.

Even back then, United's Number One, Edwin van der Sar, was already thirty-seven years old. He was a brilliant keeper, but he couldn't go on playing forever! At some point, they would need to replace him, and his replacement would need to be the best in the business.

By the start of the 2009–10 season, United had come up with a list of top young goalkeepers to watch. That list included:

Manuel Neuer at Bayern Munich,

René Adler at Bayer Leverkusen,

Sergio Romero at AZ Alkmaar,

Rui Patrício at Sporting Lisbon,

Hugo Lloris at Lyon,

Joe Hart at Manchester City,

...and, of course, David.

That was a lot of watching for United to do! Fortunately, they had scouts all over Europe. At first, the Spanish scouts saw David play at the weekends, and Eric went to any midweek matches.

So, when David came on for his Champions League debut against Porto in September 2009, United's goalkeeping coach was watching. 'Wow, how is he so calm and composed out there?' Eric wondered to himself. 'The kid's only eighteen!'

And when David saved that penalty in the UEFA Super Cup against Inter Milan in August 2010, United's goalkeeping coach was watching that time too.

'Amazing!'

With each super save that David made, Eric grew

more and more excited. Not only was he a brilliant
shot-stopper, but he even looked and played like
United's current Number One!

'He's the right guy to replace Van der Sar,' Eric
decided. His mind was made up. Now, he just had to
make it happen.

First, Eric spoke to the United's chief scout, Jim
Lawlor. As soon as Jim saw David in action, he
agreed. 'Right, let's speak to Sir Alex.'

In the United manager's office, Eric and Jim
presented a video of David's best moments – the
saves, the punches, the catches, the kicks. They
could tell that Ferguson was impressed.

'He's already playing week-in week-out for
Atlético,' Eric added, handing over all the excellent
scouting reports, 'and he's not even twenty years
old yet!'

Would David's age be a problem? No – Ferguson was
never afraid to give young players a chance. After all,
Ryan Giggs and David Beckham were still teenagers
when they won their first Premier League title.

'Ok, De Gea looks like the real deal,' the United

manager declared. 'What next?'

'Now, we need you to come and see him play, boss.'

Really? How could Ferguson do that, when
Manchester United were playing two games each
week? The manager had only ever missed one match
before, and that was for his own son's wedding!

Finding United's new Number One was important,
though. In between Schmeichel and Van der Sar,
there had been a few dodgy keepers at Old Trafford.
Ferguson didn't want any more disasters like that.

'Okay, how about 22 September?' he suggested.
That weekend, United would be playing Scunthorpe
in the third round of the League Cup, so if he *had* to
miss one match, that was a good one to pick.

Eric checked the Atlético fixture list. 'Perfect,
they're playing Valencia that day!'

That night in the Mestalla Stadium, Eric and Sir
Alex took their seats to watch the David de Gea Show.

A header from Aritz Aduriz... SAVE!

A shot from Juan Mata... SAVE!

At the final whistle, Ferguson smiled and nodded
to Eric: 'Yes, that's the guy we need!'

United still took their time, however. What was the rush? They had to be 100 per cent sure before they bought him. Even the worst goalkeepers had a wonder-game every once in a while!

Also, David wasn't the only top young goalkeeper around. By then, their long list had been cut down to two: Neuer and David. But which one would they pick?

For the rest of the 2010–11 season, United always sent someone to watch David play.

Sometimes, it was Eric,

Sometimes, it was Jim,

Sometimes, it was Sir Alex's brother, Martin,

Sometimes, it was the first-team coach, René Meulensteen,

Sometimes, it was the assistant manager, Mike Phelan,

...And a few times, it was Ferguson himself.

But whoever it was who watched him, the report never changed – David was definitely the real deal.

'Right,' Ferguson decided eventually. 'It's time for us to make our move!'

When David heard that United had made an offer to buy him, he couldn't believe it. Yes, there had been rumours for years, but he never thought that his dream would actually come true! He felt thrilled and terrified at the same time.

'Is it too soon for me to leave Atleti?' David asked for his dad's advice. 'Van der Sar is a legend, and so is Schmeichel! How can I follow in their footsteps? I'm only twenty!'

José put his arm around his son's shoulders. 'I know you're ready for this.'

On 29 June 2011, the deal was done. David signed for Manchester United for around £18 million. He was now the most expensive goalkeeper in Premier League history, and the second most expensive in the world... EVER!

'He's an outstanding replacement for Van der Sar,' Ferguson told the media with a big smile on his face.

Yes, David had a lot to live up to as he arrived in Manchester. Wearing a red T-shirt, he stood next to Sir Alex, holding up a yellow United goalkeeper shirt. It was almost as bright as Schmeichel's shirt in that 1999 Champions League Final!

'I feel very proud and I can't wait to start playing here,' David said to the translator in Spanish. He would need to start taking English lessons as soon as possible. 'I'm going to do my best to show what I can do.'

CHAPTER 15

DIFFICULT EARLY DAYS

Those first few months in Manchester were a real shock for David. The lifestyle, the language, the food, the weather – everything was so different from Madrid!

'Isn't this supposed to be summer?' David asked his dad as they sheltered from the howling wind and rain.

'Yes, son,' José shivered. 'You can say goodbye to the Spanish sunshine!'

David was very grateful that his parents had agreed to move to Manchester with him. Yet again, they had happily given up everything to look after their only child. The three of them were living together

94

in a huge house on the edge of the city. What would David have done without them? Sit at home and play PlayStation on his own, probably!

Soon, David also had his best friend back. In late July, Kun signed for United's local rivals, Manchester City.

'Man, what is this weather?' the Argentinian complained as soon as he arrived.

David laughed. 'I warned you!'

Mum, Dad and Kun: David was going to need all their love and support for the difficult days ahead. He was playing for one of the biggest clubs in the world now, and the pressure was really on to perform.

'The Premier League is a tough place for a young goalkeeper,' Eric explained to him. 'Teams are going to test you to try to find your weakness. You've got to be strong, both mentally *and* physically.'

Mentally, David was already strong. He was calm, focused and brave, and he bounced back quickly whenever he made a mistake.

Physically, however, David had work to do. He was tall, but he was still as skinny as a stick. He only weighed eleven stone, which was nothing compared to some of the big boys in the Premier League. If he tried to catch a corner-kick, they would crush him!

Eric couldn't let that happen, and so he came up with a really hard fitness programme for David. 'You're not going to like this,' he warned the goalkeeper, 'but you'll thank me one day!'

Eric was right; David didn't like it at all. He had always hated going to the gym, but suddenly he was spending hours and hours there, before and after team training.

'I'm a goalkeeper,' David groaned grumpily. He just wanted to be back in bed. 'Why do I need massive muscles?'

'Keep going!' his coach encouraged him. 'One more lift, that's it!'

David had to change his diet too. Apparently, he was eating too many tacos and not enough healthy foods.

'You're a professional footballer,' Eric told him sternly one day. 'It's time to start acting like one!'

And it was also time for David to make his United

debut. The Community Shield was always the first game of the season and it was extra special in 2011 – it was a Manchester Derby against Kun's City.

'Come on, lads!' the United captain Nemanja Vidić shouted as they walked out onto the pitch at Wembley. 'This is Trophy Number One!'

With Nemanja, Rio Ferdinand and Patrice Evra playing in front of him, David felt calm and confident in goal. They were three of the best defenders on the planet! For the first thirty minutes of the match, David hardly had anything to do.

'Keep concentrating, keep concentrating,' he told himself again and again.

However, at the end of the first half, it all went horribly wrong. When David Silva curled a free kick into the United box, David rushed off his line, but then stopped. Uh oh, why had he done that? He was never going to reach the cross and now Joleon Lescott had a free header at goal. Too late – *1–0 to City!*

David was furious with himself. 'Why, why, why?' he asked, flapping his arms in frustration.

Unfortunately, David's United debut was about
to get even worse. City striker Edin Džeko dribbled
forward and took a shot from way outside the box.
It should have been a simple save, but David didn't
dive down quickly enough. Too slow – *2–0 to City!*

Two mistakes in seven minutes – what a
nightmare! David just wanted to run away and hide,
but he didn't. He came back out for the second half,
and United came back to win.

Chris Smalling flicked on Ashley Young's free kick.
2–1!

Nani chipped the ball over Joe Hart. *2–2!*

Then, with seconds to go, Nani dribbled all the
way from the halfway line and scored again. *3–2!*

In goal, David punched the air and then wiped
his brow. Phew, what a relief! Despite his poor
performance, he had won his first trophy at United.

'Sorry boss, I'll do better next time,' David
promised his manager after the final whistle.

Ferguson patted him on the back. 'Don't worry,
you're still learning. These things happen.'

Unfortunately, they kept happening. United were

winning 1–0 against West Brom when Shane Long took a shot. David threw himself down to make the save but somehow, the ball squirmed under his arms. *1–1!*

As he watched the ball land in the back of the net, David's heart sank. No, not another mistake!

United still won the match, but that didn't matter. All anyone wanted to talk about was David's display:

'The goalie is like a jelly!'

'De Gea looks like a kid who won a competition to play in goal for Manchester United.'

Every week, the opposition team tried their best to catch him out with high balls into the box. David had good games too but, of course, people focused on the bad ones, like the 6–1 defeat to their rivals, City.

'Dodgy Keeper!' the opposition fans behind his goal cried out every time he kicked the ball.

It was such a disaster that David thought about giving up and going back to Spain. Luckily, his coaches weren't going to let him do that.

'Stay strong!' Emilio told him on the phone. 'Do

you remember your early days at Atleti? You made lots of mistakes back then and look at you now!'

'Hey, you just need to find your calmness again,' Eric told him. He was even learning Spanish to help David. 'The goalkeeper has to be the calmest player on the pitch. You're one of the coolest keepers around!'

'Don't give up now,' José told him. 'This has been your dream since you were a little boy. I know you can do this!'

His dad was right; David could do this. He just had to keep believing in himself. With lots of hard work, he would turn his United career around.

CHAPTER 16

BOUNCING BACK

Despite David's optimism and determination, the
year 2012 began with him sitting on the Manchester
United bench. After another error against Blackburn
Rovers, Ferguson decided to play Anders Lindegaard
in goal instead.

David was devastated, despite his manager's
explanation: 'You've played a lot of football already
this season. A little break will do you good.'

Really? David wanted to make up for his mistake
and he only knew one way to do that – by saving the
day. How could he do that as a substitute?

'Don't worry,' Patrice promised him. 'You'll be
back!'

Usually, Patrice's smiling face was enough to make David laugh, but not this time. Ferguson picked Anders to play against Newcastle United...

...then against Man City...

...then Bolton Wanderers...

and then Arsenal.

'I'm never going to win my place back!' David moaned to Javier 'Chicharito' Hernández. They were both on the bench, while United embarked on a winning run without them.

'If we keep working hard,' his Mexican teammate reassured him, 'our chance will come.'

David was certainly working hard on his goalkeeping in training. With Eric's help, he was focusing on one area in particular – his footwork. As well as controlling the ball and kicking it downfield, David also practised making saves with his feet.

'You use your long arms all the time,' Eric argued, 'so why not use your long legs more often?'

What a great idea! By using his legs, David found that he could stop lots more shots, especially the low ones. Now he couldn't wait to test out his new skills on the pitch for United...

Finally, his opportunity arrived. Anders was injured, so David returned to the starting line-up against Chelsea at Stamford Bridge.

'See, I told you that you'd be back!' Patrice said with a big smile in the tunnel.

This time, it worked. David felt relaxed and ready to become a United hero.

He didn't give up when he made a good save with his feet, but it bounced off Jonny Evans and into the net. *Own goal – 1–0!*

He didn't give up when his old Spanish Under-21 teammate Juan Mata scored with a vicious volley. *2–0!*

And he didn't give up even when David Luiz's header deflected in off Rio's shoulder. *3–0!*

'Come on!' David roared. 'It's still not over!'

Wayne scored one penalty, and then another. *3–2!*

Chelsea midfielder Michael Essien hit a powerful long-range strike, but David punched it away. SAVE!

'Keep going!' he clapped his gloves together and cheered.

David's teammates listened. Chicharito came on and scored a header. *3–3!*

It was one of United's best comebacks ever, but could they hold on for a draw? There were still ten minutes to go. In stoppage time, Paul Scholes fouled Luiz. *Free kick to Chelsea!*

What a way to end the game, with a deadly Spanish duel – Juan vs David. There could only be one winner...

As Juan's shot curled beautifully towards the top corner, the Chelsea fans were up on their feet, ready to celebrate.

'It's going in!' they cried. 'We've won!'

But David flew through the air like superman and stretched up his long left arm... SAVE!

'You legend!' Rio screamed as he gave his goalkeeper a big hug.

But the match still wasn't over. Gary Cahill shot for goal and... ANOTHER SAVE!

Wait, what were the fans singing? At first, David couldn't believe what he was hearing. The United supporters had made up a new song for him!

He's big, he's brave, he's Spanish Dave,
He makes big saves, he never shaves,
He's flying through the air,
Come and have a shot if you dare!

'I was so sure that free kick was going in,' Juan complained after the final whistle. 'How on earth did you save that?'

David just shrugged happily. He couldn't explain it; it was natural talent. As he walked off the pitch, he was absolutely buzzing. He wanted to keep playing!

David's big United bounceback had begun. After that, he was almost unbeatable.

He's big, he's brave, he's Spanish Dave,

He tipped a late shot over the bar as they beat Liverpool 2–1.

He makes big saves, he never shaves,

He saved with his long right leg and then his long left arm as they beat Norwich City 2–1.

He's flying through the air,

He reacted quickly to block a shot as they beat Tottenham 3–1.

Come and have a shot if you dare!

In United's last eleven league games of the season, David kept eight clean sheets.

'Now that's the *Niño* we know and love!' Emilio laughed.

Despite David's awesome displays, however, United could only finish in second place. For the first time ever, the Premier League title went to their local rivals, City. And who scored the winning goal to win the title? David's best friend, Kun!

'No, we're not friends anymore!' David joked.

After so many ups and downs, David's dramatic first season in English football was over.

'I survived!' he told Eric with a relieved smile on his face.

But really, David had done much more than just survive. He had bounced back brilliantly from his early errors and the cries of 'Dodgy Keeper!' Those critics were quiet now because David had shown both his character *and* his quality.

Next season, it would be time for the next step: 'Trophies!'

CHAPTER 17

PREMIER LEAGUE CHAMPION

As the 2012–13 season kicked off, the United players knew the task ahead of them – to take revenge on City by winning back the Premier League title.

But just in case they'd forgotten, Patrice reminded them in the dressing room before the first Manchester Derby: 'That trophy is OURS!'

United were three points ahead at the top of the table, but that lead would disappear completely if they lost to City. No, they couldn't let that happen. Ferguson had come up with a gameplan and it worked perfectly.

David cleared the ball straight to new striker Robin van Persie, who chested it down to Ashley Young.

Counter-attack! Ashley dribbled down the left wing at speed and passed to Wayne. *GOAL – 1–0!*

By half-time, United were winning 2–0, but David knew that it wasn't game over yet. City's superstars would fight back eventually.

David Silva threaded a great pass through to Carlos Tevez, who took his shot first-time... SAVE!

After diving down brilliantly, David now had to get back up. Silva was running onto the rebound... DOUBLE SAVE!

'Unbelievable from De Gea!' the TV commentator cried out.

No-one was calling David a dodgy keeper anymore. Sadly, however, he couldn't make it a terrific triple save. Yaya Touré's shot rolled just past his outstretched arm.

'Noooooooo!' David groaned. He couldn't believe it. After all his hard work, how had they still managed to score? City were back in the game.

David somehow saved a shot from Silva with his shoulder but with less than ten minutes to go, Pablo Zabaleta finally beat him. *2–2!*

'Keep going!' David clapped and cheered. He never stopped believing.

In injury time, United won a free kick just outside the City area. Robin's shot deflected off the wall and into the bottom corner. *GOAL – 3–2!*

'Yessssssssss!' David jumped for joy with his fists flying everywhere. As his ten teammates raced over to the corner flag, he stayed in his penalty area and celebrated on his own. But once the final whistle blew, he joined the big United party.

'What a win!'

'We played like Champions today!'

'City might as well hand us the title back now!'

There was still a long way to go, however – twenty-two games, in fact. United would need a lot more of David's great goalkeeping.

Away at Tottenham, Clint Dempsey was through on goal, with only United's Number One to beat. Surely, he would score, but no, at the very last second, David stretched out his long right leg. SAVE!

Away at Fulham, John Arne Riise's fierce half-volley was dipping into the roof of the net, but no, David stretched up his long right arm. SAVE!

With Wayne and Robin scoring the goals, and David saving the day, United raced away at the top of the Premier League. But what about the Champions League? Could they win that too?

In the Round of 16, they faced David's old Madrid rivals, Real. He was competing with his hero Casillas yet again.

'Bring it on!' David declared confidently. He had improved so much since his Atleti days. Now, it was time for him to prove it, back home in Spain.

At the Bernabeu, Real had nineteen shots, but they only scored one goal. That was because David was almost unbeatable.

Mesut Özil struck his shot with plenty of power… SAVE!

Fábio Coentrão snuck in at the back post. Surely, he would score, but no, somehow David managed to keep it out with his foot. SAVE!

Ángel Di María aimed for one bottom corner… SAVE!

Then Gonzalo Higuaín aimed for the other...
ANOTHER SAVE!

He's big, he's brave, he's Spanish Dave...

At the final whistle, the United fans stood to clap their superstar stopper. What a performance! The match finished 1–1 and that was all thanks to David.

'Man, how many saves did you make in the end?' Casillas asked as they hugged on the pitch. 'Ten? Twelve? I lost count!'

Ferguson was very impressed too. 'The boy is walking now,' the United manager announced with a smile.

'That's right!' David agreed proudly. The skinny, twenty-year-old kid who had first arrived in Manchester was now all grown up, and he was still getting better and better.

Unfortunately, the second leg at Old Trafford didn't go so well for David and his teammates. Real were just too strong, especially after Nani's red card. United were out of the Champions League but at least they still had the Premier League trophy to fight for.

'Come on, let's win it in style!' Ferguson urged his disappointed players.

Every victory took them closer and closer to the title, until at last, in April, it was only one win away. All they had to do was beat Aston Villa, and they would be crowned the new Premier League champions.

For most of the match, David was just an excited spectator.

Ryan Giggs crossed to Robin. *1–0!*

Wayne played a long ball over the top and Robin volleyed it home. *2–0!*

Ryan set up Robin again to complete his hat-trick. *3–0!*

United were so nearly there now. What could David do to help his team? He desperately wanted to win his first league title and keep another clean sheet too.

At last, David was called into action. Christian Benteke hit a low shot towards goal... SAVE!

A few minutes later, it was all over. Manchester United were the Premier League Champions!

'We did it!' David cheered, throwing his arm around Jonny's shoulder.

What an amazing team effort! David ran around the pitch hugging each and every United player: Rio and Patrice, Ryan and Michael Carrick, Wayne and Robin, Chicharito and Danny Welbeck. David had learned so much from each and every one of them.

The whole squad jumped up and down together in front of the jubilant United fans.

Campeones, Campeones, Olé! Olé! Olé!

It was a night that David would never, ever forget. And even amid all the excitement, he still remembered to run over and thank Eric.

'I really couldn't have done this without you!' he admitted, his voice full of emotion again.

David's second season at United had been a dream come true. He was even named in the Premier League Team of the Year, alongside Rio, Michael and Robin. Yes, David was well on his way to becoming a great goalkeeper.

CHAPTER 18

MORE SUCCESS WITH SPAIN

Was Del Bosque watching his super saves for Manchester United? David hoped so, but for now, Casillas was still Spain's Number One. Behind him, Valdés was still Number Two, and Reina was still Number Three.

It was very frustrating, but David could understand the manager's decision. Why would he want to change such a successful squad? Spain were the best team in the world! They had won three major tournaments in a row: Euro 2008, the 2010 World Cup *and* Euro 2012.

David was definitely getting closer, however. In May 2012, Del Bosque had called him up for two friendlies against Serbia and China. Although he didn't get to play in either match, David was putting pressure on Valdés and Reina. They both went to Euro 2012 ahead of him, but would they still be around for the next World Cup in 2014?

Instead of sitting on the bench at Euro 2012, David got to represent his country at the Olympics in London. He couldn't wait. This time, he was Spain's first-choice keeper, and he would even get to play one match at his home club stadium, Old Trafford. Unfortunately, it turned out to be a total disaster; Spain were knocked out in the first round after losing to Japan and Honduras.

After that experience, David felt further away from the senior squad than ever. He had to keep believing in himself, however, just like always.

'If you were English,' his United goalkeeping coach Eric teased him, 'you'd be an international by now. Easy!'

David laughed. 'Thanks but no thanks! I want to win trophies, so I think I'll wait for my chance with Spain.'

He just had to be patient. David was a whole ten years younger than Casillas. In fact, he was still young enough to qualify for Spain's squad for the 2013 UEFA European Under-21 Championship.

'Of course, I'll play,' he told the manager, Julen Lopetegui. 'I want to win it again!'

David wasn't the only player in the team who had already won the trophy in 2011. Thiago was back too, and so were Martín Montoya and Iker Muniain. They were the senior stars now, leading their country's next great generation.

'This time, I want the Best Player Award too!' Thiago declared. He had scored an amazing goal in the 2011 final, but the prize had gone to Juan instead.

For David, there were more familiar faces. His Spain Under-17 teammate Nacho was there in defence, and his former Atleti teammate Koke was there in midfield. And their third-choice keeper? His old youth team rival, Joel! The friends were reunited and ready to win in Israel.

Spain stormed all the way through to the final, and

David didn't concede a single goal. *1–0, 1–0, 3–0, 3–0!*

'Come on, at least let me have one shot to save!' he joked with Nacho.

But actually, David had been busy, especially against the Netherlands.

Mike van der Hoorn was through, one-on-one, but he stretched out his long right leg. SAVE!

Memphis Depay's fierce free kick was heading for the top corner, but he stretched out his long right arm. SAVE!

'David was sensational,' Lopetegui said afterwards.

Could David now make it five clean sheets out of five, and go the whole tournament without conceding a goal? That was his target, but it wouldn't be easy. Spain's last opponents were Italy. They too were unbeaten, and they had lots of excellent attackers: Marco Verratti, Lorenzo Insigne, Ciro Immobile, Manolo Gabbiadini...

'No problem,' David said in his usual calm way. Nothing really scared him, and especially not strikers!

The final, however, turned out to be a goal-fest.

Thiago scored first for Spain, but Italy fought back straight away. Immobile chased after the ball and lobbed it over David's long arms. *1–1!*

That was it; David's run of clean sheets was over. Oh well – winning the tournament was the important thing anyway.

'Don't let him escape like that again!' David shouted at his defenders.

He didn't shout very often, so when he did, his teammates always listened. By half-time, it was 3–1 to Spain and Thiago had a hat-trick.

'Come on!' David roared passionately, throwing his arms up in the air.

Only one goal conceded in nearly 500 minutes of play – that would be a pretty good goalkeeping record for a tournament. But just when David was feeling happier, Italy scored another goal. Fabio Borini played a one-two with Immobile and fired a shot into the bottom corner. *4–2!*

It was a really good strike, but David still thought he should have done better. 'Too slow!' he told himself sternly. He had very high standards.

Ten minutes later, it was all over. Spain were the Under-21 European Champions again!

Back in 2011, David had jumped for joy at the final whistle but this time, he was a bit calmer. He just clapped his gloves together and hugged his teammates.

'We did it,' Thiago cheered, 'AGAIN!'

He won the Best Player Award, while David was named the tournament's top keeper. Surely, now, Spain's senior manager would come calling for him?

CHAPTER 19

A GREAT GOALKEEPER

In the summer of 2013, as David returned to
Manchester following his success with Spain, he
found that everything was changing at Old Trafford.
After twenty-six years of winning trophies, Ferguson
had decided to retire as United manager.

The fans and players were all in total shock:

'No way, I thought Sir Alex would go on forever!'

'Uh oh we're in big trouble – who could ever
replace a legend like Fergie?'

The answer to that question would be former
Everton boss, David Moyes.

It was a scary new era for the Manchester

United players. Not only did they have a brand-new manager, but they also had brand-new coaches. First, Mike Phelan left, then René Meulensteen, and then Eric too. David was devastated.

'What am I going to do without you?' he asked Eric worriedly. His goalkeeping coach had done so much to help him.

Eric smiled. 'Don't worry, you're a great goalkeeper now!'

At tough times like that, United needed their stars to stand strong. That meant Robin and Wayne in attack, Ryan and Michael in midfield, Rio and Nemanja in defence, and David in goal. No, he wasn't a new kid anymore. This would be his third season in England.

Out on the pitch, everything was fine at first. They won the Community Shield and they thrashed Swansea City 4–1 in their first match of the 2013–14 Premier League season.

'That's it!' their captain Nemanja cheered. 'We're the same old United!'

After that, however, things soon started to go

wrong. They lost 1–0 to Liverpool and then 4–1 to their rivals, City. 4–1? It was so humiliating!

What made it even worse for David was that his best friend Kun scored twice in that Derby. When Kun's second goal went in, David jumped up and screamed at his defenders:

'Who was marking Agüero?'

Rio, Nemanja and Patrice just stood there, stunned. Uh oh, if David had to shout, then United were in serious trouble. Their great goalkeeper was going to have to step up and save the day.

Against Sunderland, United found themselves losing again. Fortunately, their Number One was there to keep them in the game. A cross came in and Emanuele Giaccherini headed the ball powerfully towards the top corner. The Sunderland fans behind the goal jumped up to celebrate – they were about to go 2–0 up.

'Not so fast!' David decided. He flew through the air like Superman and stretched out his long right arm. SAVE!

'What?' the Sunderland fans groaned in disbelief.

'How did he reach that? That keeper must be a magician or something!'

United bounced back to win 2–1, and they had David to thank for that.

'That's one of the best saves I've ever seen in the Premier League,' Schmeichel said afterwards.

Wow, what an honour to hear that from your childhood hero! And a couple of weeks later, David saved the day again with his amazing saves when United faced Stoke City.

In the penalty area, Peter Crouch chested the ball down to Jonathan Walters, who struck a fierce shot at goal. David had no time to react but somehow... SAVE!

United bounced back to win 3–2, and they had David to thank for that too.

In the Champions League Round of 16, in February 2014, Olympiakos arrived at Old Trafford with a two-goal advantage, and it nearly became three.

Their striker headed the ball goalwards, but David dived down to block it with his feet. SAVE!

However, United weren't clear of danger yet.
The rebound fell to another Olympiakos attacker,
who aimed for the bottom corner. But David slid
across his goal and stretched out his long right leg...
DOUBLE SAVE!

'Amazing from De Gea!' the commentator cried
out on TV.

Again, United bounced back to win 3–2 and yet
again, they had David to thank for that.

The team as a whole may have been struggling,
but their keeper certainly wasn't. In fact, David was
on the best form of his life.

'He's up there with the best goalkeepers in the
world!' his teammate Phil Jones declared.

David had become United's ultimate hero. At the
end of the season, he was named the club's Players'
Player of the Year *and* the Fans' Player of the Year.
He had been the one bright spark in a dark season.

He's big, he's brave, he's Spanish Dave...

'I'm very happy to win these awards,' he said
in his speech. 'We'll do our best to improve next
season.'

By the time that next season began, the Dutchman Louis van Gaal was the new manager at Old Trafford. But even with a new manager, David was still the same old David.

In fact, he felt more settled than ever at United. Not only was he playing his best football at the club, but David was now playing alongside two of his old Spain Under-21 teammates. Juan had moved from Chelsea and Ander had arrived from Athletic Bilbao.

'*Mis amigos!*' David welcomed his friends warmly. They were going to have a great time together.

United were 1–0 up against Everton when they conceded a penalty. Up stepped Leighton Baines, one of the best in the business. He had scored all fourteen of his Premier League spot-kicks so far. The Everton left-back was up against another penalty hero, however. David was determined to stop him. As a goalkeeper, this was his time to shine.

Baines ran up and at the very last second, David dived down low and used his strong right arm to block the ball... SAVE!

'Thanks, mate!' Luke Shaw said, looking mightily relieved.

David was delighted but he didn't show it. 'No problem,' he replied calmly. He was just doing his job and it wasn't done yet.

In the last ten minutes, Everton attacked again and again. Leon Osman tried to steer his shot out of David's reach, but he stretched out that long right arm again. SAVE!

Then right at the end, Bryan Oviedo thought that he had finally grabbed the equaliser. His shot flew towards the top corner like an arrow... but so did David's long left arm. SAVE!

'What a hero!' Robin shouted to his great goalkeeper.

As he lay there recovering on the grass, David allowed himself a little smile. It was definitely one of his best performances ever, although admittedly there were just so many to choose from. Like any true United hero, David saved his very best for when Liverpool came to Old Trafford.

Adam Lallana slipped a pass through to Raheem Sterling in the penalty area. SAVE with his leg!

Sterling dribbled into the box again. SAVE with his arm!

Early in the second half, Michael made a mistake and the ball rolled straight through to Sterling. The winger was one-on-one with David again…

This time, he tried to go around the United keeper, but no, there was no way past him. SAVE with his foot!

What could Sterling do? He set up Mario Balotelli instead, who hit his shot first time… SAVE with both hands!

The Liverpool players couldn't believe it. Was there a great wall in front of the goal? No, just a great goalkeeper! At the other end, United scored three goals, but David was still easily their man of the match.

'Unbelievable!' said Van Gaal.

United legend Gary Neville summed it up perfectly. 'De Gea has now become a great goalkeeper.'

CHAPTER 20

COMPETING WITH CASILLAS

While becoming a great goalkeeper at United, David had also finally become a senior Spanish international. At last!

Ahead of the 2014 World Cup in Brazil, Del Bosque called together a group of the country's thirty best players, just like he had back in 2010. This time, however, there were only three goalkeepers in the group:

Casillas, of course...

Reina...

And David!

'Mum, Dad, I made it!' David told his parents happily.

Each country had to have three keepers in their squad, so it was official; David was off to his first World Cup!

At first, Marivi and José were too emotional and excited to even speak. Their son would soon be a senior Spanish international footballer – it was a dream come true, the greatest news they'd ever heard!

Eventually, they managed to say a few words to their son:

'What an achievement! We're so proud of you.'

'Congratulations, you've worked so hard for this!'

David wasn't getting carried away, though. He knew that Casillas was still Spain's Number One, and Reina was still Number Two. He knew that he was the third-choice keeper, and so he probably wouldn't get to play at the World Cup. It would still be an amazing experience, however, and it was all part of the plan.

'By 2018, I'll be ready to replace Casillas!' he told his United teammate Juan, who was also in the World Cup squad.

Before the tournament began, Spain played a couple of warm-up matches. Reina started the first against Bolivia, and Casillas started the second against El Salvador.

What about David, though? He watched both games from the bench, but with ten minutes to go against El Salvador, he came on as a substitute.

'Good luck!' Casillas said to him as the keepers hugged on the touchline.

'Thanks!'

This was it – David was making his Spain debut! On the inside, he was buzzing with adrenaline, but you couldn't tell because on the outside, he looked as calm as ever.

'I hope I get to make a super save,' David thought to himself as he took up his position between the posts. But unfortunately, there was only time for one simple catch and roll-out. It was a start, though, at least.

'Just you wait until I play the full ninety minutes,' he told his good friend Koke at the final whistle. 'I'm going to show the world what I can do!'

That wouldn't happen at the 2014 World Cup, however.

Casillas was the keeper for the first match against the Netherlands. When Spain took the lead, the nation breathed a sigh of relief. David and the other subs clapped on the sidelines. Good – after winning the World Cup in 2010 and the Euros in 2012, it was going to be another great tournament for *La Roja*.

But no, just before half-time, Robin van Persie – David's teammate at United – lobbed Casillas with a heroic diving header. 1–1!

Spain were in shock, and the Netherlands took full advantage, as Robin and Arjen Robben in particular ran riot.

2–1, 3–1, 4–1... 5–1!

David couldn't believe what he was watching. What were the defenders doing? And what had happened to Casillas? He was usually so reliable, but he was having a nightmare against the Netherlands.

As the cross came in, Casillas jumped up to catch

it but missed the ball completely. GOAL!

When Sergio Ramos passed it back to him, Casillas took a terrible first touch and gave it straight to Robin. GOAL!

Uh oh, Spain were in big trouble. If they were going to make it through to the next round, things had to change and fast.

For the next match, against Chile, Del Bosque decided to drop Gerard Piqué and Xavi, but he kept Casillas in goal.

Alexis Sánchez's free kick was curling towards the bottom corner, but it looked like a safe save for Spain's keeper. However, instead of catching it, Casillas chose to punch it... straight to Charles Aránguiz. *2–0 to Chile!*

Spain, the reigning World Cup champions, were out of the tournament after only two matches. What a disaster!

For their final game against Australia, Casillas was out... and Reina was in. David was pleased for his teammate, but he couldn't help feeling a little disappointed. After all, their World Cup was already over, so why weren't Spain looking to the future instead?

He didn't have to wait too long, though – just two months, in fact. In Spain's first game after the World Cup, David played in goal from the start. It was only a friendly against France, but that didn't matter to him. He felt so proud standing there in line with his teammates to sing the national anthem. A big brass band played the tune behind them, stirring up the Spanish passion.

'Come on!' their captain, Sergio Ramos, cheered.

After many years as the nation's Number One, it was now Casillas's turn to sit and watch. And it was David's time to shine.

Karim Benzema was the first to test him. SAVE!

Next came Paul Pogba. SAVE!

Benzema tried again, with plenty more power. ANOTHER SAVE!

So far so good – but there was nothing that David could do to stop Loïc Rémy's wonderstrike. The ball whizzed past him before he could even react. *1–0 to France!*

Sadly, that turned out to be the final score. David's full debut had ended in defeat, but at least he was pleased with his own performance. He hadn't put a foot, or glove, wrong all game.

Casillas now had real competition for Spain's Number 1 shirt.

CHAPTER 21

MOVING BACK TO MADRID?

Was David the right keeper to replace Casillas for club, as well as country? That was the question everyone was asking during the summer of 2015, because, after twenty-five amazing years at Real Madrid, Casillas had decided to move on and play for Porto.

So, who would be Real's new Number One? Their reserve keeper, Keylor Navas, was very good, but was he good enough to be a *Galáctico*? A club like Real Madrid needed to have superstars in every position.

Real's president, Florentino Pérez, knew the superstar keeper that the club needed. He was Spanish and he had been almost unbeatable at the Bernabeu a few years earlier.

'Let's bring De Gea back to Madrid!' he decided.

At Manchester United, David had become not only a great goalkeeper, but the best goalkeeper in the whole of England. At the end of the 2014–15 season, he won almost every prize possible:

Manchester United Players' Player of the Year,
Manchester United Fans' Player of the Year,
Premier League Save of the Season,
and Premier League Goalkeeper of the Year!

David was even shortlisted for the PFA Players' Player of the Year and Young Player of the Year awards. His name was there next to Premier League legends like Eden Hazard, Alexis Sánchez, Philippe Coutinho and Harry Kane.

It was good to see a goalie getting the glory for once! Yes, David had come a very long way since those early 'Dodgy Keeper' days. He was now United's ultimate hero, the most important player in the team.

'Please don't leave!' the United fans begged.

David had a difficult decision to make. As much
as he loved playing in the Premier League, he still
missed Spain a lot. Madrid was his home and if
Real were offering him the chance to return, then it
would be hard to say no.

'But wouldn't the Atlético fans hate you if you
joined their biggest rivals?' Wayne asked. He was
doing his best to keep David at Old Trafford.

'They'd understand,' David replied with a shrug.

When he signed for United back in 2011, David
had dreamed of winning all the top trophies.
Schmeichel had done it and so had Van der Sar, and
so would he. However, four years later, all David had
was the 2012–13 Premier League title. Other than
the Community Shield, United hadn't won anything
since Fergie left.

2013–14? Nothing!

2014–15? Nothing!

During David's four years at United, Real had won
the Spanish Cup, the Spanish League, the Champions
League *and* the FIFA Club World Cup. So, why
wouldn't David want to play for them if he could?

In July 2015, Pérez claimed that the deal was done, but in fact the transfer talks went on and on and on. When the new Premier League season started, David still didn't know if he was staying or going. It was all so unsettling, for him and for the team.

'Let's just wait and see what happens when the transfer window closes,' Van Gaal, the United manager told him. Until the end of August, David wouldn't even be on the bench.

Finally, it looked like everything had been agreed. Real would give United £29 million, plus their reserve keeper, Keylor.

'Just in time!' David thought. But when he was all set to wave England goodbye, he found out that there was a problem. A big problem. The deal had missed the deadline by two minutes.

'Two minutes?' David repeated. He couldn't believe what he was hearing from his agent. 'Surely, that doesn't matter if it's two minutes late?'

But apparently it did. Until the next transfer window opened in January 2016, David wasn't going anywhere. He was disappointed but he didn't sit around sulking. There was nothing he could do, except get on with playing football for United.

'Coach, I'm ready to return,' he told Van Gaal after signing a new four-year contract. In his first game back, David made three super saves as United beat Liverpool 3–1.

'We're so glad you stayed!' Juan and Ander hugged him at full-time. 'Don't worry, we'll win a trophy this season for sure.'

Despite David's great goalkeeping, that trophy wasn't going to be the Premier League title. The best United could hope for was a Top Four finish.

It wasn't going to be the Champions League either, or the Europa League. They were knocked out of both competitions.

The League Cup? No, United lost to Middlesbrough in the fourth round.

Okay – so it would have to be the FA Cup, then. When United made it through to the semi-finals at Wembley, the players started to believe.

'Come on, we're only one win away from the final!' Wayne told his teammates before kick-off.

David was determined to get there. United were even playing against one of his favourite opponents, Everton. He couldn't wait to put on another shot-stopping masterclass. Maybe he would get to save another Leighton Baines penalty...

The referee did point to the spot, but it wasn't Baines who stepped up to take it. Instead, it was Everton's star striker, Romelu Lukaku.

No problem – David didn't care about that. It was still his time to shine.

As Lukaku ran up, David raised his arms high and wide above his head. Wherever the striker aimed, he would reach it. At the very last second, he dived down low and used his strong right arm to block the shot... SAVE!

'You hero!' Michael shouted, pumping his fists with passion.

United never gave up. In the very last minute of the match, Anthony Martial dribbled through and scored the winner. They were into the FA Cup Final!

'Yes!' David threw his arms up triumphantly. Another trophy was in sight.

In the dressing room before the final, the United players were full of nervous energy. They danced, and jumped, and shook, and shouted. Not David, though. He just sat there, feeling quietly confident.

'Don't worry,' he said, 'we can't lose. If they shoot, they won't score because I'm in goal.'

That was enough to settle everyone down. With David at the back, they were bound to win!

Even when Crystal Palace took the lead, the United players kept their faith.

Wayne crossed from the left and Juan volleyed it in. *1–1!*

Then in extra-time, Jesse Lingard smashed in an unstoppable shot. *2–1!*

David kept his focus right until the final whistle, and then it was trophy time. United had won the FA Cup!

United! United! United!

As champagne and confetti filled the air, David celebrated with his beloved teammates.

Campeones, Campeones, Olé! Olé! Olé!

He didn't take his gloves off until he finally had the

trophy in his grasp. Compared to a football, it felt so heavy in his hands!

Later on, David walked around the Wembley pitch, enjoying the moment with Juan. 'Maybe staying in Manchester wasn't so bad after all!' he joked.

CHAPTER 22

EURO 2016

Spain bounced back quickly after their World Cup disaster. In the qualifiers for Euro 2016, they won nine games out of ten.

'See!' Sergio shouted when Spain booked their place at the tournament in France. 'We're still one of the best teams around!'

Unfortunately for David, the revolution hadn't really started yet. Despite their poor performances in Brazil, Del Bosque stuck with his experienced stars – David Silva and Andrés in attack, Sergio and Gerard in defence, and Casillas in goal.

Casillas was still Spain's captain and their first-choice keeper. Of the ten qualifiers, Casillas started

seven and David started three. In those three games,
however, David kept three clean sheets.

He made Luxembourg lose,

He made Macedonia mad,

And then he upped his game against Ukraine.

In the Ukraine game, Artem Kravets sprinted past
the Spanish defence and into the penalty area. He
tried to slide the ball into the bottom corner, but
David stretched out his long left leg. SAVE!

Kravets stood there with his head in his hands. He
was sure that he would score.

Ruslan Rotan hit a vicious volley, but this time,
David stretched out his long right leg. SAVE!

'What?' Rotan screamed up at the sky. 'How did
he stop that?'

Spain won 1–0, thanks to their super-keeper. With
displays like that, David was putting real pressure on
Casillas.

'De Gea deserves to be our Number One now!'
many fans argued.

At Euro 2016, Casillas wore '1' and David wore
'13'. However, for Spain's first match against the

Czech Republic, it was David who started in goal.

Finally, his big opportunity had arrived! It was a massive moment, but David didn't panic. He had played in lots of big games before – for Atleti, for Manchester United, and for the Spain Under-17s and Under-21s. This was no different. He had been preparing to play at Euro 2016 all his life.

In the Czech Republic game, David didn't have much to do but he kept himself busy. He was always watching, moving, talking, and organising his defence. Sometimes, the defence passed to him, and he passed the ball back. It all helped to keep David focused for when his nation really needed him...

Tomáš Necid shot from the edge of the box, but David caught it comfortably. SAVE!

Roman Hubník slid across the grass to poke the ball goalwards, but David threw his body down. SAVE!

Vladimír Darida got plenty of power on his strike, but David punched it away. SAVE!

David kept a clean sheet and in the eighty-seventh

minute, Gerard scored a header to give Spain the victory. It was a perfect start to Euro 2016.

'Good game,' the opposition goalkeeper, Petr Čech, said to David after the game. They knew each other well from the Premier League battles between Manchester United and Chelsea. 'Casillas won't win his place back after that!'

He was right; David was in goal again for Spain's second match against Turkey. Del Bosque believed in him, and he believed in himself. He was a great goalkeeper now, one of the best in the world.

David didn't have much to do against Turkey, but he was always ready to help out as Spain's last defender. He wasn't a full-on sweeper keeper like Manuel Neuer, but he was still very good with his feet. As he liked to remind his teammates, he had been a star striker once upon a time!

When the ball flew over Sergio's head, David rushed out of this box to clear it away.

'Nice one!' Gerard said, giving him a high-five.

The game finished Spain 3, Turkey 0. Job done! David was delighted. His team was through to the

Round of 16, and he had his fifth international clean sheet in a row.

'Man, you're unbeatable!' Spain's left-back, Jordi Alba, declared.

But in their last group game, Croatia was the team that stopped David's clean sheet... and they did it twice!

The game marked the worst performance of his international career so far. With Spain already through to the next round, David had made the mistake of letting his focus slip.

The first time he was distracted, he got away with it. Gerard passed back to his keeper, but David took his eye off the bobbling ball. His first touch was terrible and before he could take a second, the Croatian striker raced in to steal it. Fortunately, the shot bounced back off the crossbar and into David's gloves. *Phew!*

Gerard didn't need to say a word; a look was enough.

'Come on – concentrate!' David shouted at himself.

There was nothing that he could do to stop Croatia's first goal, but he should have done better for the second. From wide on the left, Ivan Perišić somehow managed to beat David at his near post. Instead of stretching out a long arm, he stretched out a long leg and missed the ball completely. What a disastrous decision!

'Sorry!' David shouted to Sergio.

As he lay there on the grass, his shoulders slumped. Was that the end of his tournament? Would Del Bosque bring Casillas back? No, the Spain manager wasn't ready to replace David just yet.

'We can't blame De Gea for the goals,' he told the media firmly.

David breathed a big sigh of relief. He would get a second chance against Italy in the Round of 16. This time, he wouldn't let his focus slip for a second.

Spain needed David to be at his best because the Italians attacked again and again.

Graziano Pellè's header was going in, but he dived down with his long left arm. SAVE!

Giaccherini's overhead kick was going in too, but

he pushed it onto the post and away. SAVE!

David managed to save Éder's free-kick too but unfortunately, he couldn't reach the rebound. *1–0 to Italy!*

'Nooooo!' he shouted, kicking the ball away in fury.

Uh oh, Spain were really struggling. David had to be a one-man shot-stopping machine.

He flew through the air to tip another Giaccherini strike over the bar. SAVE!

He made himself as big and tall as possible to block Éder's shot. SAVE!

Italy won 2–0 in the end, but it would have been a lot more if it hadn't been for David. He could hold his head high as he clapped the Spanish fans in the stadium. He had proved himself as their new Number One.

David's Euro 2016 was over, but his international career was only just beginning. Soon, it would be time for Spain to move on to their next top target – the 2018 World Cup.

CHAPTER 23

MOURINHO'S MAIN MAN

One day during Euro 2016, David got a phone call from an unknown number. 'Hello?' he answered.

It was José Mourinho, his new manager at Manchester United. 'I just wanted to wish you good luck for the tournament. We've got a great season ahead of us. Together, we're going to take United back to the top, and win lots of trophies. You're going to be my main man, David!'

Mourinho was desperate to keep his star player at the club. Real Madrid were still trying to sign him, so what could he do to make David stay? He had an idea. In July, United announced their new goalkeeping coach… Emilio!

David, of course, was delighted. He couldn't wait to work with his Atleti mentor again.

'Don't think that I'm going to take it easy on you,' Emilio said with a smile. 'You're a great goalkeeper, but you can still get better!'

Challenge accepted; David was ready to take his game to an even higher level.

It was clear that Mourinho meant business too. As well as Emilio, he had also brought in two new superstars: Paul Pogba and Zlatan Ibrahimović.

'Okay, maybe we can win the Premier League title again!' David thought to himself.

United started the 2016–17 season well. They won the Community Shield and then their first three leagues games too. The fans dared to dream, but there was a big test coming up – the Manchester Derby! Despite some super saves from David, City won 2–1 at Old Trafford.

United's Premier League title hopes soon slipped away, but there were other trophies up for grabs. In Mourinho's first season, his team made it all the way to two cup finals.

First, David got the chance to complete his English trophy hat-trick: the Premier League, the FA Cup, and now the League Cup.

When United went 2–0 up against Southampton at Wembley, it looked like game over. But just before half-time, the Saints struck back. Manolo Gabbiadini lost his marker and nutmegged the keeper. *2–1!*

David was furious. How had his defenders allowed a striker to humiliate him like that? 'Don't you dare let that happen again!' he shouted.

But just after half-time, Gabbiadini made it 2–2. Suddenly, it was game on! The Saints kept David busy with a series of shots to save. No problem! Then at the other end, Ander crossed from the right and Zlatan headed home. *3–2 to United!*

When the final whistle blew, David punched the air. He had won another trophy! He was a cool character, though. He didn't let his excitement show. Instead, David behaved like it was no big deal. He was the last United player to climb the steps and the last to collect his medal. He took his time, high-fiving every fan along the way.

De Gea! De Gea! De Gea!
United! United! United!

'Do you ever take your gloves off?' Juan joked as
they paraded the trophy around the pitch.

David shrugged and smiled, 'You never know
when I'll next need to save the day!'

Right – one final done, one final to go. In May
2017, United faced Ajax in the Europa League
Final. David had won the competition with Atlético
back in 2010, but could he win it again? As ever,
he was feeling quietly confident. A victory would
be the perfect way to end their first season under
Mourinho. A victory would also give them a place
in next season's Champions League. David was
determined to play in Europe's top club tournament
again.

Many of United's best-ever moments had come
in the Champions League: the win over Chelsea in
2008 and, of course, the comeback in 1999, the
night when David's United dream had first begun.

'Come on, let's get back to where we belong!'

He clapped and cheered in the dressing room in Stockholm, Sweden.

For once, however, David wouldn't be there to save the day for his team. 'Good luck!' he said to Sergio Romero, United's Europa League keeper.

David watched from the bench with Jesse, Anthony, Wayne and Michael. He hated not playing, but at least his team was soon winning.

When Paul scored the first goal against Ajax, they all jumped out of their seats to celebrate with their teammates.

When Henrikh Mkhitaryan scored the second United goal, they knew that they were almost there. David spent the last few minutes standing on the touchline, waiting for the referee's whistle...

Full-time: United were the Europa League winners!

'Champions League, here we come!' David cheered as he ran onto the pitch.

There were happy scenes everywhere. Juan lifted Ander up into the air, Paul danced 'The Dab' in front of the fans, and José Mourinho Jr jumped into his dad's arms.

Although David hadn't played in the final, he still felt part of the glory. He even put on his bright green goalkeeper shirt for the trophy presentation. This time, though, he decided to leave his gloves behind on the bench. He wouldn't be needing them now.

Campeones, Campeones, Olé! Olé! Olé!

'WINNERS!' David shouted out as he posed for a selfie with Emilio.

The 2016–17 season had been a very successful one for David and his team, but the 2017–18 season was destined to be even better.

David kicked off with four clean sheets in United's first five games. The one against Basel in the Champions League was extra special because it was his hundredth for the club.

'Here's to the next hundred!' he told Emilio afterwards.

And the clean sheets kept on coming:

Manchester United 4 Everton 0,

Southampton 0 Manchester United 3,

Manchester United 4 Crystal Palace 0.

At Anfield, Liverpool had nineteen shots at goal,

but they couldn't get a single one past David.

When Roberto Firmino crossed to Joël Matip, he looked certain to score. But in a flash, David stretched out his long left leg. SAVE!

It wasn't luck; it was natural instinct. He always seemed to know where the ball would go.

Thanks to their star keeper, United were still in second place, chasing their Manchester rivals City for the Premier League title. What would they do without David?

Away at Arsenal, they might have lost by six or seven goals. Instead, however, they won 3–1!

Romelu Lukaku almost scored an own goal, but he dived down to push it away. SAVE!

Alexandre Lacazette fired in a low shot, but he used his strong right arm to keep it out. SAVE!

Alexis Sánchez was about to tap in the rebound, but David jumped up to block it with his foot like a centre-back. DOUBLE SAVE!

Arsenal's shots became more and more desperate. Héctor Bellerín tried to beat him from long-range – no way!

By the final whistle, David had made fourteen
saves, the most in a Premier League match ever. And
at the end of the season, he won his first Golden
Glove award for keeping the most clean sheets in the
league – eighteen!

Mourinho was full of praise for his main man.
'David is the best goalkeeper in the world!'

CHAPTER 24

THE WORLD'S GREATEST?

Like David himself, the people of Spain were feeling quietly confident as the national team set off for the 2018 World Cup.

'We can go all the way,' many believed. 'It'll be 2010 all over again!'

Why not? Spain were one of the favourites to win. Their national team looked strong in every position. The forwards were scoring goals for fun and at the back, they still had Sergio, Gerard and 'the best goalkeeper in the world'. That's what Mourinho had said and David was determined to prove it in Russia.

Just before the World Cup began, however, the

Spanish players learned some shocking news. Their manager, Julen Lopetegui, had been fired!

What? When? How? And most importantly, WHY?

'This is crazy,' David complained, shaking his head. 'Our first match is only *three* days away!'

And that first match was against Cristiano Ronaldo's Portugal. What a disaster! Fernando Hierro, the new manager, did his best to prepare the team, but there was so little time left.

'Come on, we've got to put all of that drama behind us,' Sergio told his teammates before kick-off. With Casillas gone, he was the captain now. 'Let's just go out there and win!'

But Spain got off to the worst possible start. Cristiano dribbled into the area and tripped over Nacho's leg. *Penalty!* David did his best to put Cristiano off, but he stepped up and scored. *1–0 to Portugal!*

The Spanish fans slumped down in the seats. Was it going to be another terrible tournament for their team? No, Diego Costa scored to lift their spirits again. As half-time approached, they were playing

MATT AND TOM OLDFIELD

their best passing football. Surely, Spain would go on
and win now…

When Cristiano got the ball on the edge of the
box, he shot straight away. *Bang!* Although he got
good power on the strike, it was heading straight into
David's safe hands. That's what everyone thought
but at the last second, he let his focus slip. The ball
bounced off his gloves and into the back of the net.
2–1 to Portugal!

It was a howler, the most humiliating moment
of David's career. He sat there, staring down at the
grass, asking himself those same questions:

What? When? Why? And most importantly, HOW?

Once again, David shook his head. He couldn't
believe that he had made such a basic error; he was
meant to be the best goalkeeper in the world! There
was nothing he could do, except keep going.

'These things happen,' David told himself. 'It's
normal, it's football!'

In the second half, Diego got a second goal, and
then Nacho scored a screamer. *3–2 to Spain!*

In his penalty area, David let out a roar of relief.

Phew, his teammates had rescued him. What he wanted now was a chance to save the day and make up for his mistake.

With five minutes to go, Portugal won a free kick just outside the area. This was it – David's chance to keep out his nemesis, Cristiano.

'Move a little to the right!' David shouted, organising his wall carefully. Hopefully, they would block it but if not, he would be there to stop it.

But Cristiano ran up and hit a swerving strike around the wall and into the top corner of the net. David barely moved – there was absolutely no way that he could reach it. *3–3!*

At the final whistle, his Spanish teammates comforted him:

'Don't worry, we still believe in you!'

'You'll bounce back from this, no problem. You're the best, bro!'

The next day, David posted a message on Instagram: 'To learn to succeed first you have to learn to fail.'

He had failed against Cristiano, but now he would

succeed against the rest of the world.

In their next two games, Spain beat Iran and then drew with Morocco. That was enough to send them through to the Round of 16.

'Right, we really need to raise our game to the next level now,' Hierro warned his players in the dressing room. It was going to be a very tough game against the tournament hosts, Russia. They defended well and they also had the home crowd on their side.

The score was 1–1 at half-time...

1–1 at full-time...

and still 1-1 at the end of extra-time!

The Spanish players passed and passed but they just couldn't find a way through. It was so frustrating to watch, especially for David in goal.

'Come on, SHOOT!' he shouted again and again, but his teammates weren't listening.

Now, the match would be decided on penalties. Could David be Spain's spot-kick hero, just like he had been for the Under-17s and the Under-21s? He clapped his gloves together confidently. It was his time to shine.

Fyodor Smolov stepped up... and scored!

Unfortunately for David, so did Sergei Ignashevich, and Aleksandr Golovin,

and Denis Cheryshev.

Koke and Iago Aspas both missed from the spot. Spain's World Cup was over, and the fans were furious. They wanted someone to blame and David was one of the players they picked.

'What's happened to De Gea? He was rubbish in Russia!'

'He only made one save in four whole games. He shouldn't be our Number One anymore!'

David tried to ignore the cruel comments, but it wasn't easy. He had lost a lot of confidence in his goalkeeping. Maybe he wasn't the world's greatest, after all.

'Hey, it wasn't all your fault,' Emilio reassured him when he returned to Manchester United. 'Yes, you could have done better with a few of those shots, but what about your defence? They didn't exactly help you, did they?'

That was true but it didn't take away the pain

and disappointment. When the new Premier League season started, David didn't make any more big mistakes, but he wasn't saving the day for United like usual.

'Last season, I would have stopped that!' he complained to his dad, his first and most important goalkeeping coach.

'Nonsense! You're getting better and better,' José told him, trying to build his confidence back up.

David had suffered setbacks before – at Atleti, and during those early 'Dodgy Keeper!' days at United – but he bounced back every time. José knew that his son was a lot tougher than he looked.

It took time but eventually, David did find his best form again. Against Tottenham at Wembley, 'The Great Wall' was back at last. He was absolutely unbeatable.

Harry Kane... SAVE!

Dele Alli... SAVE!

Christian Eriksen... SAVE!

Son Heung-min... SAVE!

Toby Alderweireld... SAVE!

Kane again… SAVE again!

At the final whistle, David had made eleven super saves to go with a clean sheet, a man of the match award and, most importantly of all, another United victory.

'That's more like it!' he smiled to himself, giving Emilio a big thumbs-up.

It was great to hear the fans singing his song again:

He's big, he's brave, he's Spanish Dave,
He makes big saves, he never shaves,
He's flying through the air,
Come and have a shot if you dare!

David's teammates raced over to hug and thank their heroic keeper.

'I've never seen anything like it,' Juan said, still in shock at what he'd just seen. 'If you ask me, there's no doubt about it – you *are* the world's greatest!'

Atlético Madrid

🏆 UEFA Europa League: 2009–10

🏆 UEFA Super Cup: 2010

Manchester United

🏆 Premier League: 2012–13

🏆 FA Cup: 2015–16

🏆 League Cup: 2016–17

🏆 UEFA Europa League: 2016–17

Spain

🏆 UEFA European Under-17 Championship: 2007

🏆 UEFA European Under-21 Championship: 2011, 2013

Individual

🏆 UEFA European Under-21 Championship Team of the Tournament: 2011, 2013

🏆 PFA Premier League Team of the Year: 2012–13, 2014–15, 2015–16, 2016–17, 2017–18

🏆 Manchester United Players' Player of the Year: 2013–14, 2014–15, 2017–18

🏆 Manchester United Fans' Player of the Year: 2013–14, 2014–15, 2015–16, 2017–18

🏆 Match of the Day Save of the Season: 2012–13, 2013–14, 2014–15, 2015–16, 2017–18

🏆 Premier League Golden Glove: 2017–18

DE GEA

1 **THE FACTS**

NAME: DAVID DE GEA
QUINTANA

DATE OF BIRTH:
7 November 1990

AGE: 28

PLACE OF BIRTH:
Madrid

NATIONALITY: Spanish

BEST FRIEND: Juan Mata &
Ander Herrera

CURRENT CLUB: Manchester United

POSITION: CM

THE STATS

Height (cm):	**192**
Club appearances:	**461**
Club goals:	**0**
Club trophies:	**6**
International appearances:	**38**
International goals:	**0**
International trophies:	**0**
Ballon d'Ors:	**0**

★ ★ ★ **HERO RATING: 89** ★ ★ ★

GREATEST MOMENTS

Type and search the web links to see the magic for yourself!

13 MAY 2007,
SPAIN 1–0 ENGLAND

https://www.uefa.com/under17/history/season=2007/

The UEFA European Under-17 Championship was David's first top trophy. His best performance came in the semi-final against Belgium. He saved the eighth penalty in the shoot-out to become Spain's spot-kick hero. Manchester United were already watching him. (You'll need to create an account on the UEFA website to watch this one!)

3 OCTOBER 2009, ATLÉTICO MADRID 2–1 REAL ZARAGOZA

https://www.youtube.com/watch?v=qkcgPwGM1Ow

Three days after his Atleti debut, David started his first Spanish League game at his home stadium. However, his childhood dream nearly turned into a nightmare. After twenty minutes, he raced out and gave away a penalty. Uh oh, could David make up his mistake? Yes, he dived down low to his left and… SAVE! The fans chanted his name; he was already an Atleti hero.

13 FEBRUARY 2013, REAL MADRID 1–1 MANCHESTER UNITED

https://www.youtube.com/watch?v=3_zRaJEevDM

At United, David bounced back from his difficult early days to become a great goalkeeper. In this Champions League match at the Bernabeu, he was almost unbeatable. David saved the day for his team again and again and again. Real's keeper, Iker Casillas, was impressed and so was their club president, Florentino Pérez.

2 DECEMBER 2017, ARSENAL 1–3 MANCHESTER UNITED

https://www.youtube.com/watch?v=ixRmRPmcxk8

In this match, David equalled the record for the most saves in a Premier League match – fourteen! Some of them were quite simple but some of them were sensational. The best of the bunch was a double save to deny Alexandre Lacazette and then Alexis Sánchez. 'David is the best goalkeeper in the world!' said his Manchester United manager, José Mourinho.

13 JANUARY 2019, TOTTENHAM 0–1 MANCHESTER UNITED

https://www.youtube.com/watch?v=SX1nL09vJ2g

After a disappointing 2018 World Cup with Spain, David took a while to find his top form again at United. This was the day when everything finally clicked again. Harry Kane and co. tried and tried, but David kept out everything with his long legs. He was back to being 'The Great Wall', one of the best goalkeepers in the world.

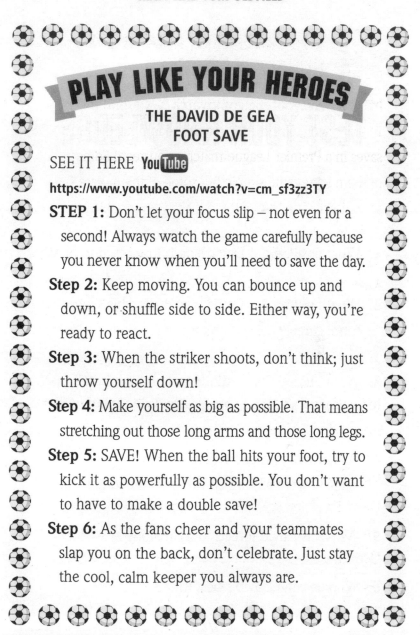

PLAY LIKE YOUR HEROES

THE DAVID DE GEA FOOT SAVE

SEE IT HERE You Tube

https://www.youtube.com/watch?v=cm_sf3zz3TY

STEP 1: Don't let your focus slip – not even for a second! Always watch the game carefully because you never know when you'll need to save the day.

Step 2: Keep moving. You can bounce up and down, or shuffle side to side. Either way, you're ready to react.

Step 3: When the striker shoots, don't think; just throw yourself down!

Step 4: Make yourself as big as possible. That means stretching out those long arms and those long legs.

Step 5: SAVE! When the ball hits your foot, try to kick it as powerfully as possible. You don't want to have to make a double save!

Step 6: As the fans cheer and your teammates slap you on the back, don't celebrate. Just stay the cool, calm keeper you always are.

TEST YOUR KNOWLEDGE

1. What position did David's dad, José, used to play?

2. What position did David play during his school futsal career?

3. What little white lie did Juan Luis Martín tell the Atlético Madrid youth coach?

4. Which two former Manchester United goal-keepers were among David's childhood heroes?

5. Why was David forced to train alone at Atlético?

6. Who became David's best friend at Atleti?

7. Which Manchester United manager brought David to Old Trafford?

8. Who coached David at both Atletico Madrid and Manchester United?

9. Which legendary goalkeeper did David replace as Spain's Number One?

10. Which club tried to take David back to Spain in 2015?

11. What's the one major club trophy that David hasn't won with Manchester United yet?

Answers below. . . No cheating!

11. *The Champions League.*
10. *Real Madrid.* 9. *Iker Casillas.* 8. *Emilio Alvarez.* 7. *Sir Alex Ferguson.* 6. *Sergio 'Kun' Agüero.* 5. *He refused to go out on loan because he felt ready to play for his favourite club.* 4. *Peter Schmeichel and Edwin van der Sar.* 3. *He said that David was about to sign for Rayo Vallecano instead.* 2. *Striker.* 1. *Goalkeeper – like father, like son!*

HAVE YOU GOT THEM ALL?

ULTIMATE FOOTBALL HEROES